THE MAN FROM SOUTH SUDAN

DENG ATAK KEN

Written by Deng Atak Ken
Copyright © 2017
ISBN: 978-0-646-96357-0

The rights of Deng Atak Ken to be identified as author of this work has been asserted by them in accordance with the copyright, Designs and Patents Act 1988

All rights reserved. No part of this publication may be reproduced, stored in or introduced into a retrieval system, or transmitted, in any form or by any means (electronic, mechanical, photocopying, recording or otherwise), without prior written permission of the writers. Any person who does any unauthorized act in relation to this publication may be liable to criminal prosecution and civil claims for damages.

This edition published by Africa World Books
www.africaworldbooks.com

Contents

Acknowledgments v
Introduction 1
My Story 3
Atak Ken Agany's Family. 5

Chapter 1
The Causes of the Conflict 9

Chapter 2
Our Trip to the Marriam. 15

Chapter 3
To Kosti 17

Chapter 4
To Khartoum 21

Chapter 5
School 29

Chapter 6
Suburbs after displacement. 39

Chapter 7
My First Love. 45

Chapter 8
Military Service - age and obligation 47

Chapter 9
Going to Egypt. 55

Chapter 10
The Ugly Side of Egypt 69

Chapter 11
My Incredible Relationship at Work 73

Chapter 12
2005 – Year of Peace 75

Chapter 13
Tribute to "martyrs;" release of POWs 81

Chapter 14
Moment for Tsunami Victims. 83

Chapter 15
An all-inclusive Sudanese State 85

Chapter 16
Moving with the momentum of 5,000 years 87

Chapter 17
National unity through pluralism and democracy 89

Chapter 18
Economic and Social Development 93

Chapter 19
Building National Consensus 97

Chapter 20
Tributes and Acknowledgements .101

Chapter 21
My Journey back to South Sudan after more than 22 years 119

Chapter 22
The Wedding Day 135

Chapter 23
Lessons for the Future 147

Adut Jok Aher 201

Photo Album 203

Acknowledgments

I'm blessed to have had extraordinary financial support from Aweil community members from people such James Wek Amoi, Malith Makc Kual and Aweil Community chairlady Abuk Ayai Akol.

Also, it will be an enormous mistake not to mention Elizabeth Sama Mayween and her husband Mr Tamim Abdelrhaman for the exceptional role they played giving me advice and motivation to be able to finish this book successfully.

I'm sure without them I would not have reached this stage. Therefore I say a big thank-you to Elizabeth Sama Mayween and her husband Mr Tamim Abdelrhaman for your outstanding help!

Thank-you also to Mr Mark Koehler for doing exceptional substantive editing work at the time this book was still on its early stages.

Thank-you also 'Love of Books' for assisting me to bring my publishing dream to life. Being on a tight budget the cost involved was more than reasonable.

Massive thanks go to my Mother Abuk Mayol Amoi and Athian Mapher Atak Ken. They didn't get a chance to assist me in the writing of this book, naturally, due to the long distance. However, they are the ones who are responsible direct or indirect for my success.

Lastly, I thank my brilliant and beautiful wife Abuk Kuach Ngor for being so graciously patient while I was writing this book. I am certain without her support and encouragement it would have for sure taken me a lot longer to get to the last chapter.

To My Dear Readers,

This is my very first book I have written.

You are welcome to provide feedback for consideration of insertion in any future book I may write.

I'm very pleased, actually delighted with my accomplishment. It wasn't an easy task at all. I chose each day not to give up on my writing with my dream goal of seeing my new book eventually launch and get published, no matter what.

Introduction

I am not famous, not a star. I don't hold a powerful position. I write my own story as a humble and simple young man who has love and great hope and passion for this magnificent world.

I am honoured to share with you my life story – the good, the hardships and the difficult moments. I am a part of God's world, and I have learnt four important lessons: First, that life is good when you have a strong purpose. Second, things happen for a reason. Third, hard work is always rewarded and fourth, when one door closes, another one opens.

I've had many setbacks and traumatic moments throughout my life, but I have been able to conquer and overcome them all with God's encouragement and by persevering.

I was born in South Sudan and I grew up in the northern sector, Khartoum. I'm writing this story for my children and the generations to follow. There will be interesting facts within the pages that they might wish to learn!

When I was a child, I dreamed of growing up and getting a good job to help my mother, to minimise her fatigue after we lost our dad.

My mother worked very hard and did so much for us. She deserves recognition. I was also keen to finish my education and work in a public service capacity in some way. I have a passion for community and social activities. I'm a good listener, and I want to be a person who delivers. I love listening to inspirational and emotional speeches. I love the truth. It is in my DNA. Sometimes my fellow South Sudanese people do not like the truth. Yes, it can be difficult and uncomfortable – yet it is the truth and it must be told.

Jesus said: 'Tell the truth, and the truth alone shall set you free.' For me then, the truth is about freedom.

This is my first book. I would appreciate any feedback. I will accept all feedback with an open heart and open mind.

My Story

My name is Deng Atak Ken. I was born In Aweil, Sudan in January 1981 before the separation of South Sudan on July 2011. Deng is a very common name in South Sudan society. It means 'rain'. My mother told me that my birth was an extremely difficult one. My birth made my entire family very worried, especially my father.

At that time, 1981, the Khartoum regime had marginalised the south of the country and there were no medical facilities for child delivery in South Sudan. This meant all mothers at that time had to give birth at home with the help of local medical people, not necessarily experienced in midwifery.

As soon as she experienced the labour pain, she told my father. It was midnight and my father went out straight away in search of a local obstetrician. However, it was a long way, a day's journey by foot. He walked throughout the night and day in terrible weather conditions. Unfortunately, when he got to the obstetrician's house she was very sick and she apologised that she could not assist.

Being resilient my father would never give up, so he continued, looking for another obstetrician. After having found the house of the next possible obstetrician she was not home.

Third time lucky thought my father as he continued to another obstetrician. When he located her, she was fighting with her neighbour out in the bad weather for some silly reason. My father was astonished! His request for help provided the opportunity to stop the fight and he urged the obstetrician to follow him back to his home.

The horrible weather got worse with heavy rain and strong winds. Difficult for them to walk forward. But with dad's determination and persistence, they managed to overcome these challenges and arrived at their destination safely.

To their happy and great surprise, my mother had already delivered a bright new baby boy without complication! Yet my dad realised that he must still pay that woman anyway, even though she had not helped with the birth. My father was a justifiable man; it was only fair.

My father told my mother that their boy should be called 'Dengit', which means 'rain' in response to his efforts even as the rainstorm continued for two more days.

He asked the family to pray for his new son. He then told them of his strong conviction 'that this boy will take care of my family after me because of the strange circumstances of his birth'.

It was a terrible situation really: no doctor, no hospital or medical supervision for the new baby as well as no birth certificate. This last problem was a common phenomenon for children born in the south around that time. This meant that many South Sudanese ended up obtaining a birth certificate at a later date. Some people were forced to choose the date of 1st January for the year of their birth. It can look quite odd to people when they discover that one third to a quarter of the South Sudanese have the same date and month for their birthdates!

Atak Ken Agany's Family

My father was known as a generous man with strong charisma. On numerous occasions; he proved how strong and resilient he was. To me, he was as one good a human being that this world has ever seen. He was a strong person in whatever he did. He established a well-respected and decent family. A family full of compassion and love that extended to the entire community. My dad adhered to the usual African culture of polygamy so he was married to four talented and beautiful women. Their names:

Akoj Kuol Baak (First)

Agam Wol Kuac (Second)

Lang Guot Morwell (Third)

Abuk Mayol Amoi (Fourth)

He taught them respect and love for themselves for Atak Ken Agany's family to prosper. They loved my father and all of us children without discrimination or favourites. Yet human jealousy can set in which is quite understandable in this situation.

I have 21 siblings as follows:

1. Garang Atak Ken. Deceased. Married Achol Diing and Anger Amok.

2. Agany Atak Ken. Known as Agany Matil. Deceased. Never married.

3. Agany Atak Ken. Known as Georgy. Married to Atong Akoyi and Amin Ngong.

4. Ken Atak Ken. Known as Ken Kamil. Married and divorced.

5. Abuk Atak Ken. Married to Dut Kuol.

6. Amiir Atak Ken. Deceased. Married Yai Anquaa.

7. Achol Atak Ken. Married to Aoh Aher Lual.

8. Ajok Atak Ken. Married to Baak Lual Baak.

9. Athain Atak Ken. Known as Athain Mapher. Married to Abuk Diing.

10. Aluel Atak Ken. Married to Garang Diing.

11. Wal Atak Ken. Married to Adut Noon Bol.

13. Bol Atak Ken. Deceased. Never Married.

14. Achai Atak Ken. Married to Garang Kenyang.

15. Ameil Atak Ken. Married to Annai Deng.

16. Amiir Atak Ken. Married to Dut.

17. Ken Atak Ken. Not married.

18. Akech Atak Ken. Married and divorced.

19. Athain Atak Ken. Known as Small Athain. Not married

20. Agany Atak Ken. Not married.

21. Ameil Atak Ken. Married to Deng Anyuon.

I feel lucky in some way because I'm the only person called Deng in Atak Ken's children. The other children had to contend with repeat names.

I'm my Mother's first born child, followed by two brothers and two sisters. In addition, we as Atak Ken's children were taught to love and respect ourselves.

My father Atak Ken Agany was a rich man with many resources such as houses, good agriculture lands and cows (used as dowry for marriage and other purposes). Without cows it was difficult to get married in Dinka society. This is why my father was able to be married many times.

I witnessed our family as strong and awesome until the Second Sudanese civil war, which started in April 1983 and reached our state in North Bahr el Ghazal, particularly Aweil North. The civil war was between the central Sudanese government and the Sudan people's Liberation Army. It was virtually a continuation of the first Sudanese civil war of 1955 to 1972.

Chapter 1

The Causes of the Conflict

There were five main causes of conflict which led to the Sudan civil war, namely:

1. The Muslim central government was determined to impose Sharia law on non-Muslim Southerners.

2. The central Government labelling Sudan as an Arab country, denying the rights of the majority to claim their African roots.

3. Large areas in the south, west and east were marginalised and disregarded from development programs.

4. The Arab Sudanese presumption that they were first class citizens, and the remaining citizens of lesser importance.

5. The absence of equality and justice in every sector of the community and country, resulting in discrimination, oppression and prosecution based on religious, race and colour.

In my own opinion, I believe that people had become furious and frustrated with the Khartoum Regime. There were stark reminders of the point clearly made by Nelson Mandela when he said, 'When a man is denied the right to live the life he believes in, he has no choice but to become an outlaw'.

Moreover, the Sudan Central government refused to acknowledge any of their mistakes. They neglected to seek a solution to make Sudan a better nation for all. Instead, they declared war against reformists such as Dr John Garang de Mabior, and against tribal regions, particularly South Sudan, where I came from.

The Central government executed intensive military operations in our region. They formed what they called 'counterinsurgency' militias such as Messeriya Arabs and Riziegat.

In 1987, many areas including my village were under intensive bombardment and troop attacks by government forces. They claimed they were pursuing the SPLA rebels.

Although only six years old at the time, I well remember the bombs and the soldiers. Mum and Dad instructed us children on what to do – to stay in one place and be quiet. We could hear the bombardment and gunfire everywhere, right to our doorstep, but eventually it stopped and we survived, thank God, and every family member was safe.

But what would happen next? Would the soldiers persist with violence against ordinary families? In the morning, we heard news of innocent people including children that had died.

Three days later we were told rumours that the Messeriya Arabs and Riziegat may begin another attack. My father advised everyone to evacuate the area immediately to avoid possible further loss of life. He suggested to the local people that they separate and go in different directions. My mother took us far away from our home near to the Arieth Market where the government army camps were based. She told me that Dad would stay around the houses to make sure no thieves came to steal from our properties. It is sad to think that some people would take advantage of others' misfortune, and jump at the opportunity to steal from others while they're on the run to save their lives. Disgusting! My father was brave and smart to think that way, but I was worried about his safety.

Chapter 1 The Causes of the Conflict

Our strategy for avoiding the Messeriya Arabs was simply to assess the situation through gathering enough information on the direction the troops were travelling, and then try to go in the opposite direction. There was no safe place, nowhere to hide; so we went to the bush. We stayed there several hours, and during that time my Mother was attentive and looking everywhere, to make sure nothing would harm us. She kept asking passers-by if there was any news on troop movements.

We sat under trees all dusty, dirty and scared, but we had no option but to stay put. We shared what little food and water we'd carried. Hours later, we saw a huge plume of smoke in the sky in the direction of our village. Later we learned that the Messeriya Arab had entered our village, and killed at random, abducted children, women and cows, pillaged, killing men and destroying properties.

We were told that they had burnt down many homes before leaving. Of course, we were frightfully worried about our dad as well as several other family members who weren't with us. We were helpless; there was nothing we could do.

We remained in the bush for one whole day. Then under the cover of darkness my mother told us kids to pack up and we'd look for a safer place to sleep. 'Don't be frightened,' she said. 'God is great and he will protect us.' We walked for about three kilometres and found a house.

My mother asked us to wait quietly while she approached the building. She talked to a woman and explained our desperate situation and asked for a room for just one night. The answer was 'yes'. It was a long night, we rested but could not sleep for worry and anxiety over our Dad and other absent family members.

In the morning, we dressed and prepared ourselves to leave. We gave a big thank you to the woman for her generosity. Mother decided we would now make our way back home.

On our return, we discovered that many houses still stood undamaged, and luckily, ours was one of these. But how eerie was the place? Homes empty, streets empty and quiet. We could see no one.

Our house was empty. Where was everybody? Then Dad appeared in the doorway and greeted us all. We all ran toward him, including my mother. Lots of hugging; it was very emotional.

Dad asked if we'd run into any Messeriya Arabs? We told him, no, luckily; that we'd hid in the bush and so forth.

'How did you survive the Messeriya attack?' 'They were here, weren't they?' Asked my mother.

'Yes, they were here, It was a miracle, God must have protected me. They came in huge numbers, some walking, others on horses. They attacked with speed and killed whomever they found. I climbed the big tree.' said Dad. He indicated the large tree next to our house that provided so much welcome shade in the summer heat.

'They passed right underneath me. I was so high up and camouflaged in that tree that they didn't see me. The soldiers ransacked and burnt houses and shot people. They brutally abducted some people and even started to torture them to get answers to questions, but I couldn't hear any of the conversations.' Dad said.

My mother prepared some food for dad because he hadn't eaten for some days. Then the rest of the family arrived home. They said they did not come across the Messeriya but they too were exhausted and hungry because their food was gone by the end of the first day away.

Dad was jubilant to see us all back home safe. He told us to be ready in case the Messeriya come back again.

Chapter 1 The Causes of the Conflict

He was right to worry – the situation was deteriorating day by day with no sign of let-up. We were forced to leave our homes every time we heard them coming. The Messeriya used that for economic purposes because they marauded everyone's properties in their absence.

Like us, the Messeriya also avoided the SPLA, because in their battles, the Messeriya usually came off second best, with heavier causalities. This was the reason they targeted only civilians.

In 1988, the Messeriya marauded our farm which was some kilometres away in a place called Pandit and stole the cows which were the source of our livelihood. It became harder for the entire family to survive.

My brother, Athain Atak Ken, was especially affected by that too. It was harder for him to swallow the loss because he grew up among these cows and he was the one who took care of them with passion and love. The cows were everything to him.

From that time, our family began to struggle economically. Since then we were never able to regain any momentum to recover from the loss of wealth and property.

I could go further and say that the Messeriya Arabs (who were the central government's counterinsurgency) resulted directly and indirectly in the collapse and devastation of South Sudan. The end result is starvation, extreme poverty and many lives lost.

After the loss of property and income, my father started to struggle to care for his four wives and their kids. Perhaps that is one of the disadvantages of being married to so many women because in times of extreme crisis recovery can be difficult.

In South Sudan, many people were displaced, and there was a large exodus. One night my Father asked everyone in the family to come together for a family discussion. He then made our dire situation clear to all.

He suggested that while he would stay, we should all get the train to Khartoum in the hope of a better future in the Sudan capital city.

Everyone agreed except for his first wife (Akuac Koul Baak) and her first-born child (Garang Atak Ken), and his third wife (Lang Gout Morwell).They would stay.

Soon we were ready to go to the train station with optimism and hope that things would be better in Khartoum. It would have been a challenge, but my Dad had somehow managed to pay for the tickets. My mother told us that we didn't have much food for the journey and that we would need to be patient.

Our dad joined us to say goodbye at the station. The train would take us only as far as Marriam which was about 145 kilometres away from where we were - at Aweil.

Inside the train, we sat down on the floor because there were no chairs left. People who had no ticket and those who could not find room inside a carriage climbed up on top of the roof – which was risky and dangerous. But what can you say; they did it because there was no other option. Thank God, all of the Atak Ken family was inside the carriage.

The train engine gave a loud signal and we were on our way to Marriam. From there we would catch a car to Kosti, the capital city of White Nile State.

Chapter 2

Our Trip to the Marriam

On our way to the city called Marriam, we sat in an overcrowded railway carriage. Movement and relaxation was very difficult, with shortages of food and water for everyone. The little ones cried.

We were anxious and worried because my mother had heard that the train might be attacked by Messeriya Arab and they would sometimes abduct children.

My mother and everyone stayed vigilant all night – no sleeping even for one minute. In the end, we arrived at our first destination safely and exhausted.

We weren't sure where to go from the train station. It was not familiar to any of us. Dilemma. We sat with some people at the train station. Nowhere to go, no shelter, and still no food or water and the place was dirty.

We were fortunate because some local residents took pity on us when they realised we were so hungry and thirsty. They informed the people at a nearby United Nations base of our plight. After one day, the UN arrived. They were absolutely awesome, because they helped us in our desperate situation. But unfortunately, some people after having empty stomachs for so long, had eaten too much too quickly. Perhaps it was too much too late, and they had died.

My mother, being strong and wise, monitored our food intake and eventually we were able to fill our stomachs.

We saw some people dying in front of us, and our mother stood up and told us to take courage and not to be frightened for with the help of God, everything would be just fine.

A few days later, my mother told us to get ready because a Luri Driver agreed to take us to the Kosti – our second destination before Khartoum. The man brought his Luri and asked us to pack our things so we could leave. We didn't have much to pack and told him, 'We are ready, are you?' He showed us some procedures and asked us to be careful of the products he was taking to Kosti. We'd be sitting on top of them and it'd be a long journey. He asked us to be patient and if we wanted to go to the toilet just inform him and he'd stop.

We jumped into the car, but I was scared because that was the first time ever for me to ride in a car. I wondered if we could trust this man to take us safely to where we intended to go.

Chapter 3

To Kosti

On our way to Kosti city, we experienced and witnessed difficulties and inconceivable moments. We were challenged by hunger and thirst every day. We also were faced the constant threat of the Messeriya Arab and Arab Riziegat, time was on their territory. Unfortunately, there was no way to make it to the safety zone, which was Kosti city and Khartoum at the time without passing through territory they controlled. A nightmare for us.

It was a miserable situation because there was no authority to stop them from doing terrible things like abduction and murder.

Every time they stopped our Luri car, they checked and searched everyone in the car. They asked insulting questions and although we understood little Arabic, we knew it to be disrespectful. We were subjected to this treatment day after day on our way to the Kosti city.

One night they stopped our car and by the light of a lamp they took three boys who just joined our group from Marriam. The boys' parents tried to stop them, but they threatened to kill the parents. Even the driver tried to intervene, but could do nothing. The boys were crying and their parents too, kneeling for help, but unfortunately, none came.

For me personally; I was terrified because I could be taken as well. My Mother Abuk Manyuol Amoi was worried and scared that maybe we could be next. The Driver was ordered to continue. We had to leave the three children because we were helpless.

Our mad and painful journey continued until we reached the City of Kosti and we thanked God, for our arrival, apart from those three boys. The boy's parents told us that they would not continue the trip to Khartoum without the children. The boys' mother said she would go to the Kosti police station and go back to find her lovely boys – she was scared but said she had nothing more to lose. She'd go back no matter what happened.

We thanked God for our safe arrival, who knows the three abducted boys could have been my brothers and me.

We thanked the Luri Car driver for being such a good human being, however fatigued and overburdened, for bringing us to Kosti city.

He thanked us and said he was disappointed for the children that been abducted by Messeriya; and that he wasn't able to help. He hoped that in God's will they will be found safe and healthy, and one day be reunited with their parents. He told us to take courage because life would be better in Khartoum. He gave us directions to the emigration field, where people like us stayed because there was no good accommodation.

When we arrived in that place, we found many people from South Sudan including the rest of the Atak Ken's family who took a different path to come to the Kosti City. It was a quick and emotional reunion; everyone started to tell his part of the story, and the difficulties. Others were crying because they lost their loved ones, including the abduction of children along the way.

For Atak Ken's family, everyone was safe, but some were very sick.

Chapter 3 To Kosti

Later we saw residents of the Kosti city coming towards us in huge numbers. They were carrying food, water, clothes, blankets and other things that we desperately needed. Me personally; even though I was a little boy I felt that the Kosti people were generous without exception. My mother and the others received this assistance as they distributed the goods to the people fairly. Everyone thanked the residents of the Kosti city for their extraordinary support and generosity.

We stayed there for some days receiving enormous help and support from the Kosti local people. As we rested, we wondered how we'd make it to the last destination.

Some other Southerners, who were there before us, visited us and they gave us encouragement. They told us that we were not alone in this burden and with God's grace, we would be all right. They provided us with a little more support, my mother and the rest thanked them and told them, that what they gave meant a lot, considering our situation.

One night, we were told by a police officer that we must evacuate the field as soon as possible. During that night, some people went out to search for their relatives or friends in the Kostis's city areas, hoping to find a place to live in.

But we knew nobody in that big city. However, some Kosti residents told us to go to the railroad and find the old train, unused and not working. There were other displaced people there and we should not be worried.

We walked for two hours to the area they described, and managed to find a space for us. We lived there for three months before making our last trip to the Sudan capital city. During that period, we received anonymous support from the United Nations after they were informed about our miserable situation.

This UN help gave people some peace of mind, and they expressed their happiness and jubilation because they were relieved from some of the anxiety and fear of the Messeriya. We were much safer.

The majority of kids took that opportunity to play some international football. Some danced and sang traditional songs that nobody would understand except us. I was grateful and pleased for the peace that we got at the end. As the time passed many people, especially adults, went shopping in the Kosti city. They explained to us how beautiful and magnificent the city was. When they said this, I got angry because my mother didn't allow me to go out, but I could see how terrific and tremendous Kosti was, particularly with all the lights at night.

While we were there some relatives in Khartoum, who knew my father personally sent us money. My mother said we would book tickets on the bus for all of us to leave this place as soon as possible.

Three days later, we left. We wondered if Khartoum would be a better life. We walked to the bus station and everyone was excited. At the bus station, our names and tickets were checked and we began our trip to Khartoum.

Chapter 4

To Khartoum

We departed with enthusiasm. The bus driver helped us with our seats and said it was over 300 kilometres to Khartoum – a long journey.

He said, 'We will not stop regularly but please feel free to let him know if we wanted to go to the toilet.'

I didn't understand, what he was saying because my Arabic at the time was terrible, but passengers informed me later. We left at ten o'clock for the Sudan capital with optimism in our hearts to find better life.

As we travelled some people slept, others were silent. I watched the spectacular view and this journey was safer than the previous ones; no one disrupted us on the road.

The driver did stop several times to give people a chance to eat, drink and go to the restroom. We reached Khartoum and the entire Atak Ken family got another bus to Klaklat Governorate, South Khartoum. We had relatives in that area. As we were waiting for our relatives to arrive we looked in a big and wonderful supermarket. Some Arab people started bullying us because of our untidy appearance. We were carrying our remaining possessions – old blankets, clothes, a cooking pot etc. When our relatives arrived, they rented another bus and took us home to where they lived, a suburb called Alqibba.

We were welcomed warmly into their home, embracing us with smiling faces. Some even cried because it had been a long time.

Food was laid out for us and they told us to eat first, and talk later. Ho! My God, I was so delighted, as I was so hungry. I started to eat and the rest of the family gradually followed.

After that, we began a long queue to have a shower because they had one bathroom only. We related the story of our difficult trip. They suggested to us to try to forget the suffering and have a good and positive life here in Khartoum. It was good counselling and motivating. Even though they did not have a lot, it was nice hospitality from them, a sign of strong unity and collaboration in our community. That night the kids slept on the floor.

In the morning, I awoke late because I was so tired. There were many people about in the morning – they'd come to visit us.

My mother encouraged me to meet all the visitors. They kept saying to me, 'Oh, you're going to be a big man in the future and help your mother. We thank God for your safe arrival.'

One woman was so kind to me; she asked me to sit down beside her and requested the tea to be brought to me. While I was drinking tea, she was chatting with me and made me feel so happy.

We met new people every day and they helped us with money and moral support. I was amazed at their kindness. The children taught me how to play international football (soccer). One day I was goalkeeper and my teammates were happy with my performance. However, near the end of the game, one of the boys kicked the ball strongly toward me and it hit me in the stomach. It knocked me unconscious. I couldn't breathe at all, and the boys laughed, not realising it could have been serious. One man saw me and realised that I needed First Aid. A few minutes later, I was back to normal, but the man was not happy with the other boys.

Chapter 4 To Khartoum

'This boy was in danger,' he said and he took me home in his car. When he told my mother about the incident and what he actually did to save my life, my mother was very grateful. The man left and after he said he didn't need that much appreciation.

My mother asked me many questions such as, 'When did you go there? Why didn't you tell me? What would I do if something happened to you?' I was silent.

In the morning, she asked me how I felt. When I told her that I'm okay, she looked at me and said, 'Inform me if you're going out again, please.'

We continued to live there for more than three months. On 30th June 1989 my mother told me that no one was allowed to go outside, but didn't say why.

Later we heard heavy bombardment. Apparently, there was a military coup-taking place in Khartoum capital. Omar Al-Bashir has come to power, assuming office through a military coup that ousted Sadig Al-Mahdi. I wondered if we were going to have to run again or what.

Several weeks later things were back to normal. Shops reopened, groceries became available, people went back to their jobs and people were in the streets again. Children were allowed to go outside.

A funny thing happened to me one day when my mother sent me to a grocery shop near to the house. She'd sent me to buy oil and sugar. The problem was that my Arabic language skills were not good, but she assumed I would be all right.

I arrived in that shop, and panicked when the shopkeeper asked me what I wanted. I told him I wanted sugar and oil, but he couldn't understand me. He kept asking me, 'What do you want?' I kept repeating myself over and over. In the end, he told me, okay led me outside the shop, and he gave me many dishes and cups to wash. I thought maybe he wants me to help, and then he will give me what I was asking for.

Three hours later, I was still washing dishes, and my mother started to get worried. She sent someone after me to find out what is going on. They found me just washing dishes and cups, and then he asked the shopkeeper what was going on?

The shopkeeper said that this boy had asked for a job and he gave him a job.

They sorted out the misunderstanding and the person apologised. He put his hand on his wallet and gave me too much money and told me, even though I had no clue about the Arabic language yet, I was a good boy, with a good heart and wished me God's grace.

Oh Jesus, when I arrived back home everyone was laughed at me for days! Oh my, how silly.

My mother was doing her best to find a job in Khartoum. She also wanted to find a suitable school for us kids. She had not had any education herself, but was adamant that we should. My older brother from another mother called Athain Atak Ken was of the same opinion and was a strong motivating force in my life. He suggested we move to be closer to the schools.

At the end of that year, 1989, we received the heartbreaking news of the death of our father, Atak Ken Agany. He was 85 years old He had witnessed the death of his first son Garang Atak Ken, which had distressed and shocked him greatly. His health had deteriorated after that.

The news was devastating to the entire family. The family announced three days of mourning. During that time, we were visited by many Aweil community members, and they stood by us. They prayed to God to have mercy on his soul. You have to take courage and move on from this desperate situation and move on, they said.

Some weeks later after we finished mourning, my mother told us to 'pick up our stuff and be ready to leave Klakla Alqibba

Chapter 4 To Khartoum

suburb and move to the Klakla Munawra – which will be better because you're going to start your schooling and I'm going to find a good job there'.

We didn't argue with my mother, just did exactly what she told us. It took us half an hour to reach our destination because the driver was driving too fast. When we arrived, we were received warmly by Aweil citizens who were living in that suburb.

But my welcoming was the exact opposite by Arabs boys. They wanted to fight me every time I went out to play soccer or was sent on an errand to the shop.

They called me John Garang, due to my Dinka background because the SPLM rebel leader, Dr.John Garang, is from my tribe (Dinka). Our battles were a contest with no clear winner. If they defeated me one day, I'd retaliate the next day. We used stones, kicking and bullying. That situation continued day in and day out until my mother approached their mothers and asked them to talk to their boys to stop this unreasonable war against me. In the end, we made peace and started to live as sons and daughters of that suburb.

One morning a woman called Sarah visited us. She asked my mother if I would be able to work with her on her garden. But my mother told her that I'm still a little boy.

'Don't worry,' Sarah said. 'Deng is like my son, and I will not let him do anything over his capacity.'

My mother agreed. After the woman left my mother explained everything to me. She told me that I must report to the woman's house every day and she will tell me exactly what I'm going to do. I did exactly what mother told me. The woman used to treat me nicely every day I showed up. She gave me money and some unwanted clothes from her own son. I was very happy to continue doing my job.

One day, Sarah's son said he could not find his shoes. His mother told him to take his time and search the house properly. I joined the search, but unfortunately, we didn't find the shoes. When his father came home from work, he accused me of stealing the shoes.

'I have not seen them,' I said. But he didn't believe me, and started to shout at me.

'If you don't tell me where they are I will take you to the police station because I'm sure you took them.'

'Please stop,' I said. 'I'm not a thief and not a bad boy.' I said if he wanted to take me to the police station, no problem.

Then his wife defended me. 'What are you doing? Deng is a good boy. Please calm down and give him a break. Don't involve yourself in this issue because you don't know these people like I do,' he said.

'These people are thieves, criminals,' he said. Then he took a big stick and tried to hit me, but I ran away. It was about time for me to go home anyway, but unfortunately, I was attacked by a big dog on my way home. It bit me and one boy came out of his house with a hammer to help.

When I reached home my mother took me to the local health clinic, but it was under-staffed and they could not help me.

In the morning, my mother went to Sarah's house and asked what exactly had happened?

She apologised and said that it was just a misunderstanding because they had found the shoes. 'I'll be delighted to see him back again and continue doing his job as normal,' she said.

But my mother was furious. 'Deng will not come back anymore. I agreed to him working for you because you said you'd look after him. Remember he's only a little boy. What did your husband do in response to him helping you with jobs? You

Chapter 4   To Khartoum

accuse my son of theft and question our integrity and dignity. Is this how your family pays back those who do a good thing and extend a good hand to you?'

'Come on Abuk you're a good woman,' said Sarah. 'Please forgive me and my family. I know you are not going to let your son work with me again but what I need from you right now is forgiveness.'

'Plus, a dog bit him as he ran home. I have to take him to the hospital tomorrow, 'mother said.

'All I ask is you to forgive me for God's sake, I beg you,' she said.

Mother told her 'no problem'. She could forgive her and she left the woman.

We went to the Khartoum teaching hospital for a series of injections over a two-week period.

On our way, out from the hospital on day, we found the Sarah and his son at the door. We were surprised to see them there.

'Our neighbour's dog bit my son on his hand badly,' she said.

'I am really sorry to hear that,' said my mother. But on our way, home mother told me to take courage because God's justice had just revealed itself. We must trust him.

My mother later visited the boy when he he'd returned from the hospital. He was okay and had to undertake a series of injections, just like me.

We finished going for the injection course together, and their family were sorry for what they did to me after they found out that I was innocent.

My mother (she is brilliant) visited the boy from time to time and until she made sure the boy was okay – which of course forced the boy's mother to come and visit me as well.

She told my mother that she was 'unbelievable, with a beautiful heart full of love and forgiveness'.

Three weeks later, we were visited by my brother Athain Atak Ken. He informed me that he had enrolled me in class one at Kamboni Shajara primary school. I would have to start in two weeks. I was so excited.

Before I started my schooling, my mother found a cleaning job. She started working three days a week. She worked very hard. Her first pay was spent buying school uniforms and educational stuff for me. She impressed her boss with her good work and soon was offered and began working five days a week.

Chapter 5

School

My first day in school. As soon as we arrived at the school, my brother Athain Mapher took me to the office and introduced me to one of the teachers. Then Athain went home.

I went for a walk around the school; everything was so big – the courtyard, even the school building. There were offices, a church building and a nun's room.

At 8.30am, the bell rang. What did that mean? It was a big morning assembly called the Tabur al-sabah I later found out. The assembly was in a circle, and one of the teachers stood in the middle and introduced himself. He asked for a volunteer to say a prayer for us on this beautiful and wonderful morning. One of the students took courage and did just that. Next, we sang our Sudanese National Anthem as follows:

Nahnu Djundullah Djundulwatan. In Da A Da Il Fida Lam Nakhun,
Natahaddal Maut Endalmihan,
Nashta Ril Madjd Bi Aghlathaman,
Hathihil Ard Lana! Falyaish Sudanuna,
Alaman Bayn Al Umam,
Ya Benissudan, Hatharamzukum;
Yah Miluleb, Wa Yahmi Ardakum.

(ENGLISH TRANSLATION)

We are the army of God and of our land;
we shall never fail when called to sacrifice.
Whether braving death, hardship or pain,
we give our lives as the price of glory.
May this land, Sudan, live long,
Showing all nations the way.
Sons of the Sudan, summoned now to serve,
Shoulder the task of preserving our country.

I was amazed and impressed by the singing, even though I didn't understand the words. The teacher talked about some school rules for the benefit of newcomers: Come to school on time, make sure you're clean, wash your clothes regularly, respect your teachers and classmate etc. He promised punishment if we did not comply. Understand?

Yes Sir, everyone responded. Then he told us to queue up for our classes, quietly.

In my class, I sat beside a boy call Garang Garang Tong, who lived in the same suburb as me. We talked about going home after today's studies. A teacher entered our classroom, and everyone stood up for him. I did the same, even though I didn't know why. A classmate later told me it is a sign of respect that students must offer.

The teacher told us to listen carefully.

'My name is Garang Mayeen, and I am a manager of this school,' he said. 'I will be your Arabic language teacher this year. Then he excused himself for a minute and brought back a stick with him, whacking his hand with it he then put it on the table. I started to get nervous. He looked each of us in the eyes and said, 'Here in this class, I have simple rules for you to follow and if you don't, you'll be in trouble:

Chapter 5   School

1. You must participate in class activities.

2. You must behave.

3. You must respect yourself and your classmate.

4. Your attendance is compulsory, and if you miss class, you will be punished, and if you continue to be absent, then you will be expelled.

He called out the class list. We would have to pass tests in the middle of the year and at the end of the year. Our first lesson was the Arabic alphabet. Then Mathematics and Religion. At 2.00 pm, the bell rang to mark the end of the school day. It was home time.

On my way home, I joined many students who were going to my suburb including my new classmate Garang Garang.

When I arrived home, my mother asked me, 'How did you find your first day at school?'

'It wasn't too bad,' I said, 'but the teacher was very strict.'

'No worries, just follow the rules and make sure you do your studies inside and outside school very well, and I'm sure you will be excellent,' my mother said.

'What about your job mother, how is it so far?' I asked.

'Fantastic! The woman is so nice to me, and that gave me a lot of motivation. It's an easy job, I just clean the house, wash dirty clothes, wash dishes and cups. A bit like the job you had Deng.' She laughed.

I went out to find some friends to play football together. I found some friends and we played and talked for about six hours. When I arrived home, my mother was worried.

'Deng where have you been? Don't you know you have school tomorrow? Come here and have a shower right now.' After the shower and dinner, I went straight to bed. I was tired.

My Second day in school

In my second day at school, everything was similar to the previous day. We did an art class. During lunch time one of my classmates told me that we must do our best to try to always be in the top ten. Everything here is very competitive, and you must work hard for it. Otherwise, you'll be (Eatish,) which means the person who comes last in the class and students will make fun of that person.

Education was not the learning experience I expected – more like avoiding punishment than learning anything. But my mother and brother Athain Atak were determined to see me go to school.

There was a lack of proper facilities such as toilets at the school – no clean water, and only one toilet so all of the students had to line up.

At 2.00pm when school finished I told friends I knew the way home and I would go home by myself. I arrived home at 3.30pm, then went to play football as usual.

My third day in school

I reached school a little bit late due to the lack of transport. The teacher asked me why I was late.

'I'm very sorry teacher,' I said, 'but it wasn't my fault because there was no bus.'

'This is not an excuse Deng – you should leave home early,' he said.

'I did, but what should I do if there's no bus?' I said.

'No, don't argue with me please,' he said. 'I'm going to punish you right now so you learn to come early tomorrow. Please extend your hand.'

Chapter 5 School

Then he hit my hand ten times with the big cane. It was so painful for me, and it was the first time I experienced school discipline, but I didn't cry because girls were watching.

My classmate sympathised with me and said: 'This guy is no good. He should let you go without punishment because you are right, there was not enough buses today.'

It was not a good day at all for me. I got another punishment in class when I failed to answer one of the maths questions. At the end of the day, I fought with one of the boys in class because he said to give him money, which I didn't have. I remember that day as Black Thursday.

The boy was much bigger than I was, but I had no option but to fight back. That person gave me a beating of a lifetime, but the good thing was that I refused to give up. I was crying yes, but I kept fighting, fighting and fighting, I had nothing to lose. I knew if I gave up today, he would do this to me repeatedly. When the boy realised that I am not going to give in easily, he went away and those who were watching, clapped for me.

When I arrived home I was exhausted, tired and starved, but unfortunately, my mother was still away. There was nothing to eat at home.

When I explained my situation to my mother after her work, she gave me some money to buy something to eat. I slowly started to feel better.

When I went out to play football, I met my brother Athain Mapher who gave me encouragement. He said I must learn to be a man, and I also want you to do well in your school, he said.

I became used to the school environment. Moreover, the boy who attacked me on my third day in school ceased to do that anymore and strangely enough, he was trying to be my friend. I declined his friendship because I wasn't happy with what he did to me and I didn't trust him.

After six months, we completed the term one test. I didn't know how to study at home, so my results were terrible. I was student number 25 out of 46, which meant I was outside the top ten. Not a good outcome, but I didn't care.

On our way, home many students were running and bullying (what they called in Arabic, Eatish) the person who got the last number in class. They called him stupid. I wondered why they should treat him that way. I tried to help, but could not. My friends told me that they do that to make that person do well next time.

At home, my mother was okay with my results I got. As long as I am not what they called 'Eatish'. I was astonished that my mother knew this term because she didn't go to school at all.

During the term one holiday, I didn't do much except play soccer and visit relatives.

The year seemed to go quickly and in the final tests in 1991 I managed to pass. Even though I found the tests very difficult, I scored number 22 of 46, so I had improved slightly.

My mother Abuk Mayol and my brother Athain Mapher congratulated me for passing class one. Athain told me he wanted me to achieve top ten in class two.

I sat for my class two in Kamboni Aezzoab, a school not far from the previous school. Again, I took the bus. It was a challenge for me because I found myself in a new environment and I was struggling to find new friends.

I managed to finish that class successfully and qualify to go to the class three.

In 1992, I was enrolled in class three in Kamboni Tariea, which was also in our area. But I wasn't able to finish that class in that year because I was hospitalised, along with my brother Ken Atak Ken, in Khartoum teaching hospital. He suffered from a severe illness.

Chapter 5   School

My mother said, 'Deng I'm really sorry I had no choice but to drop you from school so that you can stay with your brother in the hospital until he gains full recovery from his disease. I'm absolutely aware this decision will affect your progress in school, but I don't have much of an option dear.'

At that time, I was eleven years old, but I was an active and strong boy. Therefore, I knew the situation that my mother was in because she had to take care of the rest of the children. She needed me to stay with my brother for him to finish his treatment.

My mother visited us regularly at the hospital and provided whatever we needed. My brother Athain Atak also visited us every day after his work. We were also visited by some relatives including our cousin, Mr Agany Agany. During that short period I built strong relationships with doctors, nurses and patients. They loved me, and I loved them back.

There was one disagreeable incident when a racist doctor called Salumaa refused to shake my hand. It happened as we were crossing the road.

She was one of the treating doctors in charge of my brother Ken. But then a few minutes later she changed her mind and decided to greet me with her two fingers only. This was embarrassing. I couldn't figure it out, but I was told not to worry because she is just a racist and nasty Doctor. I decided not to greet her again anymore no matter what.

Another unfortunate incident occurred when the hospital security officers said that I'd stolen some clothes from a woman, even though they had no evidence, but I think they accused me because I was a black boy.

Some of the nursing staff said that I'm not a thief, but the security men refused to listen. They took me to the security office building, and they started to torture me by hitting me with a hose-pipe and stick asking me to confess.

I was crying and I prayed to God, Jesus and Mother Mary to help, because I didn't steal, and I'm not a thief. But the situation continued and I was really suffering badly from the beating. In the end, one of the security officers who knew me well entered the security building and asked them to stop beating me immediately. He told them loudly that I'm not a thief. He said I was absolutely free to go.

In the evening, I told my brother Thain Atak. He was furious when he heard my story so he took me to the security office and asked them to explain. But another security manager was there and he told my brother to calm down. Then he apologised to us, and said, 'I consider this an unprofessional act by my security officers because they didn't have enough evidence to condemn and torture this boy. By the way, we caught the thief this afternoon. I offer my sincere apologies on behalf of this department. I'm really so sorry Deng, and I promise you this type of thing will not happen again as long I'm in charge of security.'

We were powerless and we knew all Southerners were targeted and discriminated against every day by police and national security, so we decided to let it go.

Three days later my brother Ken Atak was discharged from the hospital. My mother was so happy – she'd been praying every day.

After being away from school for one year, I was back at school again. I enrolled again in class three in Kamboni Tariea and this time I was joined by my two brothers who started their first class ever.

That year was unforgettable, because I was able to find a smart and talented friend called Peter Gout Akol. He gave me motivation by telling me that I can make it into the top ten.

Chapter 5   School

'You just need to learn how to prepare for tests,' he said, 'and I'll show you how. I followed Peter's lead and slowly my academic results improved.

At the end of the year, our teacher called me as student number three in class and Peter was number one. My God, how happy I was!

From that day, I started to believe in myself, and I thanked Peter for that. So, I started to love school and look forward to it with optimism and enthusiasm. Peter said that I had the potential to be number one.

In February 1993, we were visited by Pope John Paul II, and the surrounding schools participated in the reception of the Pope at Khartoum International Airport. I was amongst many students and 10,000 Sudanese Christians waving, singing and dancing in celebration of the arrival of the Pope.

In our last class, we did three tests, and I proved that Peter's prediction was one hundred per cent right when for the first time I became student number one in our class, and Peter was number two.

I told Peter I was sorry for what happened, and that I owed him a big thank you.

'Take it easy Deng – it happens all the time and is normal my friend but be ready for the next class because the competition is now open,' he said.

'No worries,' I said.

In the following year, we move to the Klakla Abu-Adam because the owner of the house asked us to leave his house.

At the new house, we were joined by my brother Georgey Agany Atak and his lovely wife, Amin Nong Majok. In the new suburb, I found good and reliable new friends; Isaac Maniem, Riing Deng Wol, Michael Yeil Madok, Klong, Gout Gout, and

Garang Koul Mabior. Some of these friends were my classmates in Kamboni Tariea which I decided not to change although we changed our living address. The others were my soccer mates.

In the same year, which was 1994, Khartoum Islamic Government issued an unprecedented order for all displaced Southerners who were living inside Khartoum to be moved outside of the city.

The sites selected were unprepared and far from water, work and education. We southerners found ourselves targeted by the government of the Islamic regime. It was highly discriminatory. Without proper explanation, most southerners found themselves without any choice, outside of the city in unknown places such as Jpruna in North Khartoum, Jabal Awilia in South Khartoum and Sahra in eastern Khartoum.

The police used big cars to move people forcibly. To our great surprise, they didn't come to where we lived. My mother considered this as a miracle because the police and government agency searched everywhere. But with God's help they didn't enter our home, even though we were ready to leave.

We praised the Lord for not being dispatched to those miserable places without facilities. Many people, including those of my age ended up on the street, with no one taking care of them.

Many were rounded up in the markets and on the streets. Some were sent to camps and institutions run by Islamists. There were no proper procedures in place to contact their families or relatives. Some were beaten for small breaches of discipline and dispatched to camps without consultation with parents; others were given a religious (Islamic) education regardless of their background beliefs.

Some young boys were incorporated into the government militia and brainwashed into fighting against their own people in South Sudan territory.

Chapter 6

Suburbs after displacement

After the government displacement of Southerner refugees our streets became empty, and so did the churches. We all felt that the displacement was both malicious and racially motivated. We managed to let life move on but felt that there was something missing.

Many students were absent from school, including some of the teachers. I struggled to find friends to play with. However, my performance at school was still excellent, and the teachers were proud of my achievements in class.

My mother was still working with the same woman she used to work with and remained socially active in our community. We saw festivals at Christmas time, and went to the cinema to watch movies. I remember one day at the Khartoum cinema; a boy stole our money which put us in a difficult situation to get back home.

We explained to the bus driver what happened and he was very kind and allowed us to travel at no charge.

When I turned 14 years old I worked again for the second time in Klakla Lafa Shopping centre as a plastic bag seller. I normally worked on weekends, on holidays and sometimes after school if there was a chance. I managed to earn good money from that simple job and helped my mother and myself despite unacceptable behaviour from radical Muslims and racist Arabs at the shopping centre. They would not buy from me simply because of my colour and Christianity background.

For example, one day, I was shouting 'kays kays kays' in Arabic which means 'bag bag bag'. A man heard me and said, 'Yes please, bags.' That time I was walking with an Arab boy.

So immediately I ran towards the man, and I arrived there first with a smile and happy face, before the Arab boy. I thought I would get the business. Unfortunately, the man didn't buy from me. He chose to wait for the Arab boy who proudly took his time. I was disappointed and embarrassed, but this was normal. I was becoming used to it.

However, there were good people who bought bags from us who didn't care which part of Sudan we came from or what religion we were. They just wanted the bags to put their goods and stuff in. These people I relied on. I did that job for some years.

In 1995, I moved to the Kaboni Klakla Alqibba primary school because that was the only school that class six was available. However, that class was challenging because of the many subjects I found I had to deal with. My English results were horrible. The class was overcrowded with 64 students in the class. The teachers in that school loved to punish us all the time, even for a simple mistake made by one person – they took it as a chance to punish the entire class. Their rule was obvious, no mercy and no pardon.

During that class, I failed English as a subject twice. But I managed to be student number 19 of 64 in term 1, and 13 of 64 in term two. It was the first time I found myself outside the top ten in class. But thank God, I passed that class and was promoted to the next class.

I was always active and worked hard, and I didn't waste time at all. But I made a big mistake when I decided not to be a bag-seller anymore. I took that decision because I was growing up. I started to get to know girls and every time they went shopping they found me selling bags. It made me look ridiculous. Therefore, I decided to stop that job and look for an adult job.

Soon I found a construction job near to our house. They called it Munna in our local Arabic accent. I worked there for one week and then the person who employed me disappeared with my salary. On Thursday afternoon, he'd promised me he would pay me tomorrow. Because I was new to the job I accepted this without question.

The following day I waited for him, but he didn't turn up. On Monday of the following week, I went to the worksite. I found another person was in charge and he told me that the person I was looking for has no place there anymore. Apparently, he'd taken money from the owner.

'Okay, what about my money sir,' I asked.

I absolutely don't know,' he said. 'You were working with him last week?'

'Yes sir and he told me that he would bring my money but until now I'm still waiting,' I said.

He suggested I go and look for him and said he was sorry that I didn't get paid. I asked if I could work here this week but he already had enough people. I left very disheartened.

At home, my mother felt sorry for what happened to me.

'Don't worry my son, God will provide you with another job and the money, 'I know you work hard.' Said mother.

She asked what I would do next. I said I didn't know, but I will start looking tomorrow to find another job. She was proud of my optimism and determination and she kissed me on the head.

I left no stone unturned looking for work. It took me a while. With Almighty God's help I found another Munna job three weeks later. This time things were a little bit better.

The man who employed me was a good and honest man. He feared God and he took care of his workers. I was paid on time. With the money I got from that job, I gave some to my mother and kept some for my personal requirement such as clothes, shoes, school equipment and enrolment fees.

Later when school resumed, I had to quit work and started class seven in 1998. With a fresh mind, curiosity, and a lot of energy. I had a strong passion for school.

That same year there was unprecedented action by the Sudan police. They started to implement an unreasonable presidential order, which was that all churches in Khartoum be completely destroyed.

They destroyed part of the Tariea church plus other churches in Klaklat. In Klaklat Alqibba's Church was where I used to pray every Sunday.

There was strong resistance from many believers and some stayed inside our church for more than a week praying, day in and day out. Some even perched themselves on top of the church's roof. The police realised how determined we were. We demonstrated such a strong signal of disobedience and that people were ready to die to save the church. The police forces stood down fearing the seriousness of the situation.

When they left everyone danced, sang and celebrated victory and thanked God for His help. We were united more than ever. I saw Christians who don't regularly pray turn up and stand with us to defend our church. Even some Southerners we normally considered as intoxicated without a clue about Christianity. They left their drinking aside and came to help. They were ready to die with us. Even some Muslims turned up to help. With action and determination, we were able to overcome the police, even though they arrived in huge numbers with the destruction equipment. We'd taken non-violent civil disobedience and were successful.

Nineteen ninety-eight was a very busy period for me personally. I was attending school every day. I was preparing for year eight primary school examinations. I managed to do my own studies and sometimes I joined my friends and classmates and did our practice collectively. I was more focused and more determined than ever. At home, my mother was treating me well. She encouraged me when she felt I lacked motivation.

She would always say, 'Deng, do your best and leave the rest to God and trust me, God will not disappoint you. Hard work and diligence are always rewarded in the end.'

'Thank you very much, mother. How lucky I am to have a merciful, kind and courageous mother like you,' I said.

At that time, we were joined by my brother's daughter Amiir Garang Atak Ken. She offered to help me with my studies. Every day I returned from school I found everything in my home well organised by her. She also did a fantastic job in the mornings. She prepared morning tea, because in our culture boys and men are not allowed to do that sort of stuff. She also looked after all visitors.

In 1999, I sat my exams; my mother asked me not to walk around too much and visit many houses, due to the danger of the cholera disease, which spread very quickly. The disease was killing many people, and some we knew personally. Even my own little sister was affected by cholera, but she recovered quickly when we took her to the Khartoum teaching hospital.

Chapter 7

My First Love

For the first time ever, I now had a girlfriend. I was 18 years old. Her name was Abuk. She was a marvellous girl and the most beautiful girl not only in our class but also in the entire school. She accepted me straight away and I believe she'd had plenty of previous offers (though unfulfilled). I think she accepted me because I was doing very well at school. But regrettably, I ended our relationship in less than one month, for a couple of reasons. It was affecting my school performance because I couldn't stop looking at her all the time in class. I couldn't concentrate and was messing up. Also, I found I couldn't sleep at night and a lot of students were beginning to get jealous of me.

My brother and mentor Athain Atak felt that being engaged at this stage in a serious relationship with a girl was a problem. He said that girls are part of the decoration of this magnificent world, however at this early juncture you must focus on your study, your family, and your country. Education is a golden opportunity and I should take it while I have the chance.

It was sad, but I had to tell the girl. She could not agree with me for two weeks, but in the end, she did with tears in her eyes.

Slowly we both recovered and a couple of months later we sat our year 8 examinations. I was confident and I did a fantastic job in all subjects but not the English subject.

I looked for a job again while I was waiting for my results. I eventually found a job with the Khartoum City Council. I caught a bus to work and began to save money which went toward my secondary school uniform. I also gave some money to my mother.

One day, I was told by friends to go to our School because they have our results already. As soon as I heard this, I ran straight to school to collect my result. My teacher said, 'Congratulations, you got 171 of 250 which means you did a good job sir.'

I was so happy even though it wasn't the result I was looking for, but I was happy and my school achievement brought a smile and jubilation to the whole family.

My brother Athain congratulated me and asked me to keep up the momentum. A few weeks later I went to the ministry of education and collected my year eight primary school certificate. I was proud and delighted to have that certificate in my hand. Shortly after I was accepted into the Klakla Tariea High School.

Chapter 8

Military Service - age and obligation

In the same year, the Sudan government issued a decree asking every citizen to comply with compulsory national service. It was a 1-2 year military service obligation for every citizen aged 18-33 years, particularly the male.

They would stop buses on the road and ask for photo and age ID. If you were above 18 years of age and without a specific job they took you away. Many southerners were furious because they were intent on avoiding war and any kind of military activity. Nor did we want to go back to South Sudan and fight in our own territory and against our own brothers and sisters in the South.

But they wanted us to fight our own people. That was exactly what happened – particularly for those who had been forced to go to the South as military personnel.

People would run away when they saw the police and buses from the Khartoum capital would be stopped.

But I had my school ID which was acceptable for them at that time; students did not have to enlist. Yet the whole situation was bizarre.

In 2000 to 2001 I completed my first two years of Secondary studies in Klakla Tariea High school with distinction. Not only was I in the top ten, but I was also the top student during the two years I spent at that school. For us Southerners it was the first time we found ourselves sitting side by side with students from the whole part of the country of Sudan after we had been marginalised. But they appreciated how talented we were we as students from the South. It was a great opportunity for us.

During that time, we did an outstanding job after we managed to be in the first top ten in all the classes which was an incredible achievement. Me personally, I did an unbelievable and exceptional job in all my subjects. My classmates thought of me as an excellent and clever student, even from another planet.

I remember one North student asked me: 'Deng, can I be like you one day and achieve a remarkable result at a school like you?'

'Yes, you can sir,' I said. 'What you need is to engage yourself in hard work at school and at home as well. I was an average student before like you, but I made a strong dedication and commitment to achieve. Therefore, you can do that also. Just let me know when you are ready and I can show you the way.'

But unfortunately, he was a lazy student and he didn't come back to me again.

Our teachers were amazed at our academic achievements during that period. One of the teachers by the name of Ali, stood in our class and said, 'My dear Southerner students; I thank you so much for your magnificent and outstanding academic achievement. With very few facilities at home. I know some of you don't even have electric light at home, like Deng Atak, but you still manage to do excellently and become top class students. I know that some of you after the school must go to work to support yourselves. Some of you are without parents, but are still able to perform very well at school. You are proof that what you need is just an opportunity to thrive. With all they

Chapter 8 Military Service - age and obligation

have, our North students come up short, and cannot make it to the top. Once again, many congratulations my dear students. Keep up the dedication.'

Wow! What honest and admiring words from Ali. Yes, he was right as I didn't have electricity at home and was using a candle at night.

It was a year of jubilation too because my brother Athain got married to a beautiful girl called Abuk Diing. We attended the joyful wedding, the happiest time since we'd lost our father and other family members in the civil war.

Athain's wife proved her true worth – she was strong, courageous, friendly and a hard worker. Most importantly she loved her new family. In a short period, she had earned everyone's respect and silenced any doubters.

Even though Sudan was our own country, there was no justice and equality. The Arab/Islamic government would look to such things as skin colour, religious practice and geographical background as matters of importance. We Southerners were treated as third class citizens.

The system was bizarre because the entire country was racist and discriminatory. Those who were Arab-Muslim were first class citizens. Those who were non-Arab, but still Muslim were second class citizens. Christians and non-religious people, including Southerners were third class citizens. They called us 'eubayd' in Arabic which meant slaves.

That was my environment for almost 14 years. All government institutions were organised in this manner. If you are Arab and Muslim you were valued and appreciated and more likely to get a job.

It forced a lot of southerners to join Islam. But not because they were a believer in Islam, it was the only way for them to make a good life for their children. With respect, some people took Islam as their sincere religious choice.

Those who kept their dignity and lived by their principles suffered a lot.

As southerners we experienced a high level of discrimination and injustice in our daily life. For example, one day my classmates and I we were coming back from school. On our way home we noticed beautiful women going from door to door vaccinating all the children. When we approached them to be included in the program, they said no, not if you are southerners.

Yet Sudanese people in general are decent people in the world. They are known for their kindness and generosity. They look after each other in good and in difficult moments. They love greeting each other with intimacy and kindness. They greet neighbours warmly and with affection. They provide mutual help all the time.

Imagine, even water is put outside the doors, called (qullah) in Arabic or Crock in English if I'm not mistaken. You can drink this water freely with confidence if you are thirsty. Meals are readily shared, by using the word 'Tafaddal' which means please enter and you are welcome to eat something. You can eat without feeling scared that maybe something will happen to your stomach afterwards. Even intermarriage is allowed among the Sudanese people. But Arab and Muslim people do not condone this unless you relinquish and abandon your religion and enter Islam to be a Muslim. They do have the most beautiful girls but I will not change my Christian religion no matter what.

In 2002, I changed my school for the last time to the private school called Raja Private High Secondary School. To do this I had worked hard during my school holidays and saved some money.

Chapter 8 Military Service - age and obligation

That year I sat secondary school examinations. We had been given a lot of options; either to choose scientific subjects such as physics, chemistry and mathematics or literary subjects like history, geography etc.

First of all, I was confused, and I wasn't sure what I wanted to be in the future. Moreover, I was good at both paths: literary and scientific. But I was struggling to find my real passion. In the end, I made a big mistake and choose scientific subjects. It was more formidable and sounded very smooth when I said it.

Every Friday we went to our previous school, Kamboni Alqibba to attend Christianity religious lessons because they didn't teach that subject in our current school. I kept working hard consistently every day until the examination day. A few months later we received our results. My results weren't that good, but I managed to pass with 64.7%. My highest mark was Christianity religious studies with 93 out of 100. But unfortunately, I didn't pass the English with only 45 out of 100; which meant a university would not accept my admission application. I needed to have passed all four subjects: Arabic, Mathematics, Religion and English. My first option available was to apply to those universities who didn't bother too much about English. But these were limited. My second option was to repeat the class and wait for another year to do another secondary examination.

There was one big complication. It was state policy that any student finishing high secondary school was required to do two years national service in the army before they enter a university. To make the matter worse, in the armed forces I could end up disabled or even killed.

Even if I did finish two years military service without injuries or disabilities, it would be difficult to pursue a career or re-enter the education system. I considered the military a miserable path to take, especially if I had to fight in the south where I was born. I still had my grandmother living there. I would rather die in Khartoum than fight my own people in South Sudan. It was a big problem.

I had passed yes, but with results that weren't good enough and my family were anxious about my future. I suffered inside and my mind was struggling to figure out what to do. How had it all gone wrong despite the hard work?

Sometimes I blame myself and sometimes I blame my God, which was unacceptable. I blamed God with regret.

I was contemplating and meditating every day to find a way out of my situation. My mother stood by me. She always used to tell me: 'Think wisely Deng, remember God's ways are not human's ways, He will have a strong reason but no one knows, only God knows. Take courage and be strong to fulfil your destiny and I have a great hope yours will be a remarkable one.'

A few weeks later I reported to the National Service office. I pretended that I had severe pain in both legs; that I'm not physically fit at all. Thank God their medical checking facilities were very poor and they believed what I told them. They did a quick appearance check and told me I was in category B, which meant I would still do national service but no military training now; and I could continue with my studies and they would let me know when and how I'd be called upon for service.

Category B people were often employed in different industries and worked for free, and the salaries paid to the government. My mother was so delighted I had avoided national service, for now at least.

One night my brother Athain visited us. He said the family were all behind me. He suggested for me to leave this country and go to Egypt and finish my studies there because the national services people would not leave me alone. I accepted, but wondered how I would get there?

Chapter 8 Military Service - age and obligation

'No worries,' he said, 'just get a good job and save some money and my wife and I will secure your passage.

I worked in construction and Sudatel jobs in different locations.

Some months later, I left Khartoum to look for work in the Kosti City again for the second time. The first time was when I was coming from South Sudan. We went there to seek Sudatel jobs and I was joined there by Wal Atak Ken and Deng Garang Atak.

We had been there for several days, but unfortunately, we didn't get the job we had hoped for, so decided to come back.

At the bus station, we found it very difficult to get a ticket because we didn't have enough money. We stayed there for a whole day without food and water. In the end, the kind people of that area provided all kind of assistance and help we so desperately needed. They gave us food, water, clothes and they talked to one of the bus drivers to take us back home despite the lack of money. The driver asked us to give him the amount of money we had. He allowed us to sit and relax while he prepared to leave. I was exhausted and I slept and thanked God for his grace and the Kosti people for their decency and kindness. When we arrived home, I told my mother everything, particularly about the goodness and kind-heartedness of the population of Kosti.

A few weeks later, I found a construction job in our area. I worked hard and saved some money. After three months, I informed both Athain Atak and my mother Abuk Mayol that I was ready to go and they gave me their final blessing.

Chapter 9

Going to Egypt

Arranging to leave Sudan to go to Egypt was a most difficult and complicated procedure. The government was deeply suspicious of Southerners because of the possibility that they might join the Sudan People's Liberation movement (SPLM) under John Garang.

The first thing I did was to secure my Sudanese passport. Then I started the process of applying for a visa from the Egyptian embassy in Khartoum. Four weeks later, I had my visa.

However, for me to exit the republic of Sudan I would need permission from the government first, especially the Department of National Service.

I reported to them and I asked them to grant me permission to leave the Sudanese territory. They refused. Instead, they asked me unreasonable questions such as, 'Why do you want to go to the Egypt? Are you planning to join SPLM?'

I told them I was going to Cairo for just a short visit, and I would be back in less than one month. I told them I was definitely not going to join the SPLM.

They then took away my passport. You are a student,' they said. 'Therefore, you have to go and do national service first before we grant you such permission.'

'Okay,' I said. 'But why did you take away my passport?'

'We will not release your passport until you bring a permission paper from the National Service Office to make sure you will not use any illegal means to exit the country, sir.'

I was shocked and I had no idea what to do next. I went back home and my mother was furious when I told her what happened. I went to my brother Athain who lived nearby and informed him about my challenges with government bureaucracy.

He told me not to get pessimistic and hopeless – we would sort this out. He said I should go with Georgy Agany to see my uncle Dhieu Mathok Diing Wol, who was a minister of peace. He should be able to help.

The following day Georgy and I did just that. But unfortunately, he said he couldn't help. In fact, he discouraged me to go to Egypt. Nevertheless, providing I could somehow get my passport, he said he'd be able to help with the process of getting to Egypt.

Three days later I summoned the courage to go to the National Service Office once more and asked if they would return my passport, but the answer was no. I left their office and I sat outside crying. I didn't know what to do. I had reached an impasse. It was the first time in my life I lost hope.

But God was smiling upon me and a friend passed by and saw me sitting down alone with a broken heart. His name was Marko Maker and he asked me why I was there. He explained he could help. He knew someone who worked in the National Service Office.

I would need money however, to pay the person for him to take the risk of retrieving my passport. I agreed. He went inside and found the person very quickly, and they came out together. Marko introduced him to me and he told me that he'd already explained the situation.

Chapter 9   Going to Egypt

The person's name was Deng and he looked like a good man.

'Do you have 150 Sudanese Dinar?' he asked.

'Yes,' I said, 'what I need is my passport as well as permission to exit the country.'

He said he could do both and that this country is systemically corrupt. He was happy to make things better for fragile people like myself.

After I had given him the money, he asked me to wait.

A half an hour later he called me to come in and do the paperwork. My God I couldn't believe it!

The whole thing took only 15 minutes and I came out with both my passport and permission to go to Egypt. It was an absolute marvel. I swear that was exactly what happened.

I was jubilant and delighted. My mother joined me in rejoicing when I told her. I felt the most energetic I'd ever been and finished all my arrangements in just one week. I booked my ticket to go to Halfa city, which was the border checkpoint between the republic of the Sudan and the Arab Republic of Egypt. I would first take the train, and then a steamboat to Egypt.

The night before I left Sudan many friends and family visited me. The celebration was unforgettable, and was organised by Athain's wife, Abuk Diing. I owe her a big thank you.

We continued until midnight and afterward I did not sleep. I was both overjoyed and worried what the future might hold for me in Egypt.

In the morning as I got ready to leave, my uncle said, 'Deng I can see how anxious you are but don't worry because wherever you go there will be an opportunity. I wish you the best and may God protect you.'

Before my mother left to go to work, she said, 'Deng My son, from the bottom of my heart I wish you all the best and crucial success in your life. Remember you have my heart and prayers and you are not alone; your great and invincible God will be there for you also.'

I left the house with Amiir Garang Atak, Athain and his wife on 1 July 2003.

We took a bus to the train station and arrived at 9 am. Two hours later the train was ready to leave. Athain gave me a phone number for our sister Achi Atak ken, and our first cousin Agany Agany. 'As soon as you arrive in Cairo,' he said, 'please contact them so they can come and pick you up. Take care, have faith. I'm sure you will manage because you're strong and clever and that makes you special. I have full confidence in that you will not let us down. God is with you.'

The train moved away from the station slowly and I couldn't hold back my tears. I was leaving my entire family behind.

I sat alone and quiet as I left Khartoum city behind. The train was very old. Three hours later it stopped due to a mechanical problem. Everyone complained about the terrible delays. An hour later, it started to run again, but that scenario kept repeating itself many times until we reached Halfa city 24 hours later.

I was tired and fatigued from sitting in one place for so long. I rented a hotel room for a couple of hours to freshen up. My clothes were dirty and full of dust because we were travelling through desert. I washed my clothes and put new clothes on.

At 6 pm I was on the steamboat and I was a little bit scared – coming from a desert country I was not used to being so close to the water. In the dark, I could just make out the heavy, heaving water. Some people I had met told me that it was normal to feel this way. They suggested trying to get some sleep and I thanked them for their advice. I then said I'll be fine.

Chapter 9 Going to Egypt

The following day we arrived in Aswan Port in Egypt. Hard to believe that I was finally there.

As I took a small bus into Cairo city and the Abbasiya Church on the way, I observed many beautiful buildings. The streets and shops were well-decorated and designed. It was like a fantasy. The whole place was wonderful and well established and we were all impressed.

The bus stopped in the front of a shop and the driver said we could get out to buy food and drinks and relax. After half an hour, we were back inside the bus again and the driver made sure everyone was on the bus.

The Abbasiya Church was a place for Southern Sudanese to meet. It was cool and quiet with incredible light everywhere.

I called my sister Achi Atak Ken by using one of the community phones. She said she was on her way. When she arrived, we recognised each other immediately and she greeted me warmly. Then she requested a taxi for us, and we went to her home.

I was greeted by my brother in law Garang Kenyang and their little kids. It meant a lot to me because I'm a humble person and I appreciate whatever I get.

My sister phoned our first cousin Mr Agany Agany, her friends and neighbours and informed them about my surprise arrival. They also joined us in such a brotherly, intimate and terrific atmosphere. They were happy to have me there.

My brother-in-law Garang Kenyang said he would take me to Mr Agany Agany's residence in Hay Aleasier. We took a small bus and I discovered he was living with his two wives and his brother Athain Agany.

As we entered his house they welcomed me warmly and made me feel at home. Agany Agany's family asked me for all the news on how everyone is doing back home. We stayed there for a whole day and discussed many critical issues concerning my future in Egypt.

It is very difficult to study in Egypt if you don't have a source of income. Agany Agany suggested that I apply to the United Nations for refugee status to be admitted to Australia.

In doing so I would become a resident in one of the best countries in the world and have a good chance to finish my study (and at the same time, support my mother). But first I'd need to write my case to the UN in order for them to assess my situation. I agreed.

Visiting his house was very helpful and beneficial to me – a great source of information and advice. Soon after, he took me to someone who was renowned for writing up such cases as mine.

I submitted my application to the United Nations branch in Egypt a few days later. I was granted an appointment for an interview with a UN officer, but it would not be for another three months.

During that time, I familiarised myself with Egypt and my new environment. I looked for a job to support myself and mother at home.

Where I lived, I was doing fantastic with everyone and they wanted to know information about Sudan.

One day an Egyptian police officer informed us that Athain Atak who is well known as small Athain had been hospitalised after they found him bleeding and unconsciousness on the side of the road. On investigation, we found that a car had hit him and the driver had disappeared.

At the hospital, we found him in a critical condition. He couldn't say a word. We stayed for some hours before the doctors asked us to leave. They told us that they needed just one person to stay with small Athain to look after him, so I volunteered myself.

Chapter 9 Going to Egypt

Later on, the doctor informed me that they had no option but to operate on Athain's knee. They needed family consent. So I called Achi and updated her and she then told me to sign the consent form.

Three hours later he was in the operating room. I started to pray to Almighty God to make the operation successful. It was successful and in the afternoon Achi visited us and thanked the doctors for a job well done.

I spent more than four weeks in that hospital and thanked God Athain started to improve, as his wounded knee showed signs of recovery.

To be honest, it was difficult for me at the hospital because I was struggling to communicate with the nursing staff. They spoke Egyptian Arabic with a local accent, which was quite different from the Sudan Arabic. But overwhelmingly I did a good job according to the doctors. My sister Achi Atak and her husband visited us regularly and provided food and drinks. In week five Athain was discharged from hospital and he later gained full recovery and was able to work once again.

I visited Mr Agany Agany's house for the third time to see how they were going. He informed me that in several weeks he and his first wife would leave Egypt for Canada. His second wife and his brother would follow them as soon as they had their visa.

He asked me to join his second wife and his brother while they're waiting for their visas. Due to the uncertainty of the visa applications and when they might arrive, he put my name on the house lease agreement, and said he'd inform the owner of the house not to give me a hard time because he would send money every month. I naively consented.

I respected him because he stood by me in my early schooling and gave me a lot of encouragement and support.

Before he left for Canada, I was able to find a cleaning job at Wonderland Disco Arena through a friend called Peter Jal who worked there. On the first day at work, the boss told me that my pay would be three hundred Egyptian pounds per month. I worked six days a week from 11 am to 11 pm and sometimes to 1 am if it was busy. It was a hard, dirty and difficult job but I had to do it to survive and support my mother financially if I could.

After Agany Agany left Egypt I moved to his house to honour our agreement. I thanked God that my new accommodation was closer to my workplace.

In February 2004, I attended an interview at UN Cairo branch. After waiting for four hours I was interviewed. I was to come back in a weeks' time to find out the outcome.

The result was that I had been accepted as UN refugee, but regrettably, I'd been given permanent residency in Egypt, which I didn't appreciate. It was not what I was looking for and I was frustrated and furious. I felt that living in Egypt meant no future, no more hope, and certainly no more school for me.

I blamed myself for the bad luck, and sometimes I blamed my God. I lost my appetite and stopped praying to God. Nothing occupied my head apart from that UN decision and what I could possibly do from here.

I informed my family about the UN decision. They felt sorry for me, but they were helpless. They told me not to give up but to keep trying and fight because life is not easy at all. When one door is closed another door opens. Be patient they said, and fill out the humanitarian application form – who knows, you could be granted a visa. Gradually my spirits lifted and I started to recover from my despondency. I moved on with my daily life.

I made the decision to keep knocking on the door to Australia and Canada, and if all my attempts were unsuccessful, then I would go back home. I would not stay in Egypt.

Chapter 9   Going to Egypt

Nonetheless I worked hard to make things better. I remembered the saying, 'what doesn't kill you makes you stronger'.

Agany's second wife Nyajok Chandit, his brother Athain Agany and I managed to create a good home environment. We helped each other and Nyajok Chandit cooked for us every day. Agany Agany did the enormous job of sending us money every month from Calgary in Canada.

For me personally, I distanced myself from the money and I didn't want to know how much he sent every month. All I said was that we have to pay the rent every month to the owner of the house to avoid putting me in trouble because my name was on the lease agreement.

One day Athain Agany and his brother's wife informed me that they had received their visas, which was awesome news. I congratulated them and I wished them a better life in Canada.

While they were organising to leave Egypt, I gave Mr Agany Agany a call to discuss my situation in their absence.

He said, 'Deng you should continue to rent the property. I was sending $150US every month for the three of you, so now I will send you $50US every month.' I told him that is magnificent. I said that Ken Athain and his wife are interested to come and live with me after your family's departure.

'No problem at all,' he said. 'This guy is a good man.' Our pleasant and smooth phone conversation ended. I then told Mr Ken Athain that it was okay for him to move in to the house.

I saw Athain Agany and his brother's wife off from the Cairo international airport, but no sooner had I returned home, I received a phone call from the owner of the house requesting his rent money for that month. I started to panic because I was not aware that they had not paid the rent.

Mr Agany Agany's brother had not fulfilled his promise to pay the rent before he left. I was completely shocked! I'd made a big mistake.

So, I told him to give me a chance until tomorrow morning, and I would get to the bottom of this and find out exactly from Mr Agany Agany what was going on. The following day I gave Mr Agany Agany a call and he told me that he sent all the money to his wife and his brother including the rent money.

Why then had they not paid the rent? I asked. He said he didn't know; but he had also sent some extra money for their journey.

Apparently, there had been much discussion about money between Mr Agany Agany and his brother and wife number two; none of which I was informed about. Mr Agany had told them to disregard the farewell party and just pay the rent, and use the rest of the money for whatever else. They hadn't listened and asked Mr Agany to pay the rent, or perhaps they would pay it when they arrived in Canada.

I had not been told any of this.

I asked Mr Agany Agany, 'now how are we going to fix this?'

'You just tell the owner of the house to wait for some days, while I wait for them to come,' he said.

'But remember I'm a victim among you guys in this situation, so please don't put me in trouble with the owner of the accommodation,' I said. That ended the talk.

I asked the owner to give me two more weeks in order, for me to pay the arrears. They had also failed to pay the electricity bill, and that made me furious, but I paid that one and I kept silent about it.

After a few weeks, I called Mr Agany for the third time. He said he'd spoken to both his brother and his wife and it seems they were not prepared to help on this issue.

Chapter 9 Going to Egypt

'What should I say to the owner?' I asked.

'I don't know man, because it was your entire fault because you shouldn't have let Athain and my wife run away with money and avoid paying the rent,' he said.

'That is absolutely a new tune from you Mr Agany Agany,' I said. 'How should I know from the beginning what money you sent to your wife?' I asked. 'Please don't put all this mess on me. It wasn't my mistake.'

We kept arguing and then I realised that Mr Agany Agany was not going to pay any more money. I said to myself, they must want me to pay this.

I took some money I had saved previously (for my mother) to pay the rent in full to the owner. However, the drama didn't stop there because we had entered another month.

I called Mr Agany for the fourth time, and he didn't pick up the phone, but his first wife did. He was sleeping, she said.

'Okay please wake him up because I need to talk to him right now,' I said. Thank God, she did just that.

I told Mr.Agany Agany that I'd paid that controversial last month's rent and now we're into another month so what now?' I asked.

'Sorry, Deng, I still don't have money,' he said.

'Okay, what about the commitment you made, the fifty every month, and this is the first month since your wife left?'

'Sorry, I don't have money man,' he replied.

I was speechless and for the first time I felt alone in Egypt, with nobody to rely on except myself. I wondered if this was a setup. A scam?

I told Ken Athain and his family what had happened, and they felt sorry for me because as it was a severe disappointment.

Many Aweil people who lived in Cairo who knew Agany Agany personally told me to take courage. All would turn out okay, they replied. Some people started to bring news from Canada. They said that when Mr Agany Agany received his brother and his second wife in Calgary he said he would not make any calls to Egypt, since he had his family.

The owner of the house began to threaten me. He told me that if I did not pay the full rent within seven days, he would kick us out from his house, take legal action and I'd go to prison.

I talked to Ken and told him that I would do my best to pay this months rent, then I would leave to go and live in Achi's house.

But I did not have enough to pay the full rent, so I informed some Aweil members about what had happened and about the threats. They asked me how much I needed, and they kindly gave me the rest of the money. I thanked them for their generosity. I still owe them a big thank-you because through their support I was relieved finally from the pressure I found myself in.

In the end, I paid the rent, and I removed my name from the lease agreement and put Ken and his family on it. I went back to Achi's house to live, and I did my best to let that tragedy go and continued going to my job every day.

Since then I have not called Agany Agany again, and he didn't call me either to ask how things went with the owner of the house.

What pains me most is that Mr Agany Agany still cannot acknowledge that he made a big mistake by promising and then not being able to deliver. He finds it very difficult to apologise. Perhaps he was confident that I would handle that difficult task successfully. Which was fine but he should have informed me from the beginning rather than commit himself to something and then not honour it. What he did to me was a huge mistake but I can forgive him; with or without an apology. After all, I took a lesson from that incident – that it is important to know a person thoroughly before sharing a financial undertaking with them.

When I was in Khartoum I knew both Agany Agany and his brother Athain Agany but I never lived with them, and that's why I paid that heavy price. I will let it go because at the end we're brothers and relatives. We definitely will need each other at some time, but I will never forget what they both did to me in Egypt. Therefore, there will be certain things I will not trust him on, no matter what. Yet I came out stronger and I was admired by the example I set. It is not what happens to us that makes the difference in our lives. What makes the difference is our attitude toward what happens.

In Achi's house, I tried to refocus on my job and forgot about Agany Agany and what he did to me. During that time, I was able to save some money and I sent some to my mother in Khartoum. I called her once a month and made sure she was doing magnificent! She always thanked me and asked me to take care.

One day my sister Achi Atak gave me an Australian humanitarian form. She told me to fill it in and try my luck. This form was sent to me by Mr Deng Jhok who lives in Australia. Achi told me that she had already submitted one form, and we were still waiting on the result. I thanked her. I went out to find someone who is specialised on how to complete that kind of form. After two days, I found someone called James who did me a favour and filled in my form after I gave him all sorts of information. I then submitted my application to the Australian Embassy in Cairo.

In all I spent 15 months and 15 days in Egypt. During that period, I experienced bad times, challenging moments and hardship. (I had almost lost hope and faith). It was a disappointing period before I was finally granted a humanitarian visa to go to the land of opportunity, the multicultural country called Australia in the year 2005.

Chapter 10

The Ugly Side of Egypt

Egypt is an incredible country in terms of infrastructure, tourism, development, education and beauty. It is a wonderful country to visit. Egyptians call it the mother of the whole world. However, it is a bit cold in the winter season.

In contrast, we South Sudanese people have been through severe racism and unacceptable discrimination. Most Egyptians do not like us because of our black skin. They resent us being in their country.

The world press and social media have failed to highlight our miserable plight and how badly we have been treated by our brothers and sisters in Egypt. For example, one Sunday morning there were three southerners going to church. Suddenly an Egyptian woman who was living in a first floor flat saw them walking along below her. She tipped a bucket of sauce on them which forced them to go back home and change their clothes. I saw that horrible incident happen, and that was a shocking moment for me. When I told this story to my sister at home, she said that Egyptian women do this all the time to southerners; and that sometimes they throw eggs. If we complained they would say: 'Oh sorry I didn't see you because you are too black to see'.

I knew an old man who told me once that an Egyptian man slapped him on his face while he was sitting and relaxing on the train. The Egyptian ran away from him and he could not catch him.

Southerners experience extreme irritation and molestation not only on public transport but everywhere they go. They call us by unacceptable and unthinkable names such 'black monkey' and 'Samara'means black.' Sometimes we will fight back. This is dangerous though because the Egyptians will join and might fight you even if you are only one person. I knew someone who was living at the same address as me, who was brutally beaten by several Egyptian youths on his last day in Egypt while he was preparing to go to the United States of America. He couldn't even walk. He took that beating just because he looked different and he is not from Egypt.

Sometimes they ask us ridiculous questions such as: Why are you here? You people overcrowd our country. Why don't you go back to where you came from? Why are you so dark? Were you put in the fire to burn?

We just listen to these questions and keep silent.

However, every day we spent in Egypt was a big challenge for us because many unexpected and unimaginable things could happen. You could be put in prison just for a simple mistake. Or you could find yourself being deported without your family or relatives even being notified.

I remember one night, I finished worked late, around 12 o'clock midnight, and I took the bus home. An Egyptian police officer stopped the bus because he saw me while he was standing at a traffic light. He entered the bus and ignored every Egyptian on the bus and targeted me.

'Hi Samara,' he said in Arabic. ('Samara' means black, an insult). 'Where are you from?'

Chapter 10   The Ugly Side of Egypt

'I'm from Shubra, Egypt,' I said.

Ha ha ha ha, everyone on that bus started to laugh. He was irritated, so he told me to get down.

'I know you are from Sudan so why did you lie to me?' he asked.

'Okay, if you are confident one hundred per cent where I am from, why did you ask me then sir,' I said.

'Now since you are being disrespectful to me, I will not let you go,' he said. 'Where is your residency document that gives you legal right to stay here Samara?'

Thank God, I was carrying my United Nations Refugee Document that allowed me to stay in Egypt. I pulled it out from my wallet and showed it to him.

When he saw it, he was speechless and couldn't go further. He said I was free to go; and that I was very lucky to have the document.

I kept silent because I was scared that he could do me harm. He'd been joined by his colleagues. When I returned to my place inside of the bus, I found all the passengers were impressed with the way I handled the situation. One person said I was smart and brave. I kept quiet until I arrived home.

Our women and girls were subject to sexual harassment every day and they were powerless to do anything about it.

The reason many southerners kept quiet on all of these issues is that we had no place to go to or any avenue of complaint. We were well-accustomed to that kind of discrimination in our own country, Sudan. In Egypt, it was worse. We were even more isolated, often without the support of fellow citizens. It was extreme racism we witnessed in a country that called itself 'the Mother of the World'.

Chapter 11

My Incredible Relationship at Work

At my work at the wonderland Disco Arena, I established a good, intimate and strong relationship with my fellow Egyptian workers. They appreciated my commitment and dedication to the job. They were impressed with my enthusiasm and optimism. In return, I thanked them and said, 'Whatever I do, I do it with love, openness, goodwill and passion.'

However, in the company of my fellow workers, it was a different world, a world of zero discrimination, racism and hatred. My fellow workers were the reason I liked Egypt most. Despite the huge challenges and racism that I had been through. They would protect me at work even if one of their Egyptian fellows misbehaved or insulted me because of the way I looked.

Egyptian girls who attended our disco every day, loved to chat with me and greeted me when they arrived. They were amazing, and I loved them back because they were beautiful girls. Even though I was doing a hard job, every day I woke up I couldn't wait to start my work.

My fellow workers encouraged me and gave me much-needed support. They assured me that one day I would leave Egypt because I do my work with such good will.

My twelve-hour workday left me with limited time to spend with the family at home. I normally did that on Sundays. Sunday was an enormous day for me. Not only to have a good time at home with the family, but I used Sunday as a day to visit friends and relatives such Ken Athain and his family. Sunday was the day that put a smile on my face when I received a letter from the Australian Embassy in Cairo to attend an interview.

In August 2004, I had my interview at the embassy with my interpreter Mr Diing Ameil because at that time I couldn't speak a single word of English. The interview took just 15 minutes. I answered all questions quickly and confidently.

I was given a medical document that meant my application had been accepted so long as I passed the medical test. Then I'd be ready to leave Egypt.

I started to see the world from a different angle, with hope and optimism for the future once again. At home, my sister Achi Atak Ken celebrated and praised the lord. She called it a miracle. At work, my Egyptian workers were very happy and said I deserved it because of my strong work ethic. From many Aweil Community members, relatives, friends and acquaintances I received congratulations. I passed the medical successfully, and now I awaited my visa.

Chapter 12

2005 - Year of Peace

January 9, 2005 was a remarkable and joyful day for South Sudanese people around the world. It was the day SPLM/SPLA under the paladin, our hero and my own role model, Martyr late Dr John Garang de Mabior and his gallant soldiers signed a comprehensive peace agreement with the oppressive Khartoum regime under the president Omar Hassan Ahmad Al–Bashir.

It was a historically significant period and a chance to bring an end to the suffering and hardship for our nation. People felt that the peace agreement would bring development to our country and our leaders would be able to consolidate a long-lasting peace not only for Southern Sudan but the entire Sudan nation.

It would take a long time for full recovery and heal. We witnessed the end of the war between the Sudan People's Liberation Army and the northern Central Government. The war had lasted from 1983 to 2005 and when it ended it was twenty-two years old. However, the elders said that it was mostly a continuation of the first Sudanese civil war from 1955 to 1972 (when Sudan gained independence).

More than two million people had died. Because of the destructive nature of war, many generations of south Sudanese had missed out on education.

The Sudan Government had committed severe human rights violations such as slavery, rape, exploitation, torture, and lack of religious freedom. They had forced people to convert to Islam against their will.

However, at the signing of the CPA ceremony, the Chairman of the SPLM/SPLA Dr John Garang gave an emotionally touching speech for the future of Sudan. He took the opportunity to articulate Sudan's problem to the world and what should be done to make Sudan a country for all. His words are always admirable, emotional and aspirational. Tears came to my eyes as I listened to his wonderful speech.

He was a strong leader for the SPLM/SPLA. During the political and military unrest, his soldiers and heavy weapons may not have reached the Khartoum capital city, but his powerful and outstanding words did.

In Naivasha, Dr John Garang gave a long and meaningful speech. I watched it from the beginning to the end. I was moved by his touching words and the rhetoric he used to entertain the gathering. I was amazed by the way he illustrated the whole Sudan problem.

His speech is as follows:

Your Excellency President Mwai Kibaki, Your Excellency former President Daniel Arap Moi, Your Excellencies heads of state and government, Your Excellencies ambassadors and representatives of the international organizations, distinguished invited guests, ladies and gentlemen, compatriots, fellow countrymen and women, allow me at the outset to convey to you my best wishes for the new year.

The year 2005 will mark the year of peace not only for the whole of Sudan but equally throughout our sub-region and Africa as a whole.

Chapter 12 2005 – Year of Peace

On this joyous day and occasion, I greet and salute the people of Sudan from Nimule in the far south to Halfa in the far north, and from Geneinah in the far west to Hamashkoreb and Port Sudan in the east. I greet and salute all the marginalised rural people in Sudan who have suffered in dignified silence for so long. I greet and salute all the farmers, workers and professionals who are the creators of wealth but who have no wealth, and who have seen their living conditions deteriorate over the years.

I greet you on the occasion of this peace, which we have just signed.

All the Sudanese women everywhere – women in Sudan, as everywhere in the world, are the marginalised of the marginalised, whose suffering goes beyond description. The Sudanese rural woman, for example, gets up at five o'clock in the morning to walk five kilometres just to get five gallons of water taking a five hour walk; spends another five hours working on the family farm and then five more hours making the family meal and then she finally goes to sleep.

I greet and salute all our students on this occasion of the peace agreement, all our youths who have borne the brunt of the 21 years of this war, and to whom the future belongs, and urge them to invest in their future and that of the nation in the post-conflict period.

Compatriots, fellow countrymen and women, congratulations - Mabruk all mabruk alaykum. Your movement, the SPLM/SPLA, and the National Congress Party government have delivered to you a comprehensive peace agreement. A just and honourable peace which we have signed today and witnessed by us all. This is the best Christmas and New Year's gift for the Sudanese people, to our region, and to Africa for 2005.

Agreement signals – second republic of the new Sudan

With this peace agreement, we have ended the longest war in Africa - 39 years of two wars since August 1955 out of 50 years of our independence; and if we add the 11 years of Anyanya II, then Sudan had been at war with itself for 49 years, which is the whole of its independence period.

With this peace agreement, the SPLM and the National Congress Party government have brought half a century of war to a dignified end - congratulations.

With this peace agreement, there will be no more bombs falling from the sky on innocent children and women. Instead of the cries of children and the wailing of women and the pain of the last 21 years of war, peace will bless us once more with hearing the happy giggling of children and the enchanting ululation of women who are excited in happiness for one reason or another.

At the political level, this agreement affirms the right of self-determination for the people of Southern Sudan and the right of popular consultation for the people of the Nuba mountains and Blue Nile. This is so that the unity of the Sudan becomes based on the free will of the people instead of on wars and the forced and false unity of the last 49 years.

This peace agreement will change the Sudan forever. Sudan cannot and will never be the same again. This peace agreement will engulf the country in democratic and fundamental transformations, instead of being engulfed in wars as it has always been for the last 184 years – since 1821. That was when our country was first invaded by outside powers and exposed to the ravages of the slave trade and predatory commerce of all sorts, and since before independence from 1955 in civil wars.

This peace agreement coincides with Sudan's 49th independence celebrations. I agree with what President Bashir said on 31 December [2004] in Naivasha, when we signed the last two documents of the comprehensive peace agreement - that Sudan's independence on 1 January 1956 was not complete because of the [word indistinct] south. The war we are ending, today first broke out in Torit on 18 August 1955. Four months before independence. The south, like other marginalised parts of the Sudan were not part of that independence. With this peace agreement, we begin the process of achieving real independence by all Sudanese people and for all the Sudanese people.

The signing of this comprehensive peace agreement thus marks the end of what I will correctly call the first republic of the whole Sudan that had lasted 49 years from 1 January 1956 to 31 December 2004, when we signed the last two agreements on a comprehensive cease-fire and implementation modalities. On a personal note, exactly 42 years to the date when I first left Sudan for the bush on 31 December 1962 to join the first war. I hope I will not go into the bush again.

This peace agreement signals the beginning of Sudan's second republic of the new Sudan. For the first time, Sudan will be a country voluntarily united in justice, honour and dignity for all its citizens regardless of their race, regardless of their religion, regardless of their gender. If the country fails to rise to this challenge of moving away from the old Sudan to the new Sudan of free and equal citizens, then the union shall be dissolved amicably and peacefully through the right of self-determination at the end the six years of the interim period.

I call on the Sudanese people to join this peace agreement, to join the SPLM and the National Congress Party in the peace process because this peace agreement belongs to them. I do not belong to John Garang or the SPLM leadership; it does not belong to [Vice-President] Ali Uthman Taha or President Al-Bashir or to the National Congress Party. This agreement belongs to all Sudan, to its neighbours, to Africa, to the Arab world and indeed to the rest of the world. That is why you see this big attendance today because this peace belongs to all of them.

Although the comprehensive peace agreement was negotiated by two parties as a matter of necessity and practicality in order to end the war. Now that the war has ended, I call on all the Sudanese people and their political forces to build consensus around this comprehensive peace agreement, and use it to end war in other parts of Sudan. We can relaunch the Sudan to the promised land of the new Sudan of progress and equality, of opportunity for all Sudanese citizens without distinction.

Chapter 13

Tribute to "martyrs;" release of POWs

Finally, and last but not least, I salute all our martyrs and all wounded heroes on both sides. I salute and congratulate all officers, NCOs and soldiers on both sides of the conflict for their heroic sacrifices. I pay tribute and thank our civil population who provided the logistics for the war, especially those in the SPLM-administered areas, for without their contribution this comprehensive peace agreement would not have been possible. It is because of the role played by our civil population in the long war that we have invited some 50 chiefs and traditional leaders representing our civil society at the grassroots. We have also invited the SPLM military band to represent the SPLA rank and file.

On this joyous occasion of the signing of the comprehensive peace agreement, as you will recall that the SPLA has always released prisoners of war, we have released so far more than 3,000 prisoners of war at various times over the last 21 years. I, here as of today, order the immediate release of all prisoners of war who are still in custody and in care of the SPLA.

Chapter 14

Moment for Tsunami Victims

It is fitting, as we celebrate this momentous historical landmark, to pause to remember the thousands of fellow human beings who recently perished in both Asia and Africa in one of the planet's worst natural disasters of the modern era.

Our hearts go out in grief and solidarity to the peoples of South-East Asia in this, their hour of tragedy in the hands of a merciless earthquake and tsunamis. We share the pain and suffering of our fellow human beings in all the countries that have been devastated by the earthquake and the accompanying tsunamis or tidal waves. We also urge the international community, after it has pledged so generously to help alleviate the suffering and rebuild shattered lives in the affected region, to spare some resources to help post-conflict Sudan recover and develop. We, therefore, look forward to a massive turnout of donors with their pledges at the prospective Oslo donor's conference for Sudan which is scheduled soon.

Chapter 15

An all-inclusive Sudanese State

Excellencies, compatriots, fellow citizens, to understand and appreciate the present historical moment of the signing of the Sudan comprehensive peace agreement, I beg your indulgence to allow me to talk briefly about the problem that we are solving now; which [Ugandan] President [Yoweri] Museveni referred to before as "the problem of people with the turbines and people with ostrich feathers."

As I said before, Sudan has been at war within itself for the whole of 49 years of its independence. We end this war today, another serious one is intensifying in the western Darfur region while another threatens in eastern Sudan.

Why? What is the problem? Why should a community subject itself to generations of war and suffering in so many parts of the country?

In our view, the attempts by various Khartoum-based regimes since 1956 to build a monolithic Arab Islamic state with the exclusion of other parameters of the Sudanese diversity constitutes the fundamental problem of the Sudan and defines the Sudanese conflict. The Sudanese state hitherto has excluded the majority of the Sudanese people from governance and therefore their marginalisation in the political, economic and social fields.

This provoked resistance by the excluded. There have been wars, and there continues to be wars in the Sudan simply because most of the Sudanese are not stakeholders in the governance.

The solution to the fundamental problem of Sudan is to involve an all-inclusive Sudanese state which will uphold the new Sudan. A new political Sudanese dispensation in which all Sudanese are equal stakeholders irrespective of their religion, irrespective of their race, tribe or gender - and if this does not work, then to look for other solutions, such as splitting the country. But we believe that a new Sudan is possible for there are many people in northern Sudan who share with us in SPLM/A, including the National Congress Party, who believe in the universal ideals of humanity, the ideals of liberty, of freedom, justice and equality, of opportunity for all Sudanese citizens.

As is the case in the south, the events in Darfur, eastern Sudan and elsewhere have made it clear that we must have an all-inclusive state at the national level and full devolution of power to the various regions of the Sudan, for otherwise; it is unlikely that the country would stand a chance of remaining united. But this all-inclusive Sudanese state which we have called the new Sudan must have some basis, for example in history that makes us one country or one nation. The question is whether there is the basis for the Sudan as a country, and my answer has also been yes, there is. That is, this affirmative answer to this question has guided us and sustained the SPLM for the last 21 years until today. For this purpose, I have always wanted to go down the corridors of history, and I want to do this very briefly. Again, begging your indulgence, and taking it for that matter - I am a guerrilla, I take my time you see.

Chapter 16

Moving with the momentum of 5,000 years

My presentation, our presentation in the SPLM is that we, the Sudanese, are indeed a historical people and that the new Sudan has an anchor in history. If we cannot find an anchor in history, then we either create one or dissolve the union peacefully. Sometimes it is necessary to go back in order to gain momentum in order to go forward. President Museveni called it something in his language. That is why you see sheep; you see rams moving backwards first when they fight. They gain momentum before they lock horns. Recently, in South-East Asia, it was noticed that the tragedy of the earthquake and the tsunamis. First, the sea receded back, and then came forward with devastating force.

We very much need to do this exercise in the Sudan. To go back thousands of years to rediscover ourselves. Gain momentum, and then move forward with the momentum of 5,000 years to propel ourselves and snatch ourselves into history once again. We have a very long history indeed. Peoples and kingdoms have lived, thrived and disappeared in the geographical area that constitutes the present modern Sudan.

Many people will be surprised that in the Bible, in the Old Testament, that Sudan was part of the Garden of Eden, where it is stated in Genesis Chapter 2, Verse 8 to 14, that the Garden of Eden was watered by four rivers. One of them is the White

Nile; it is Persian in the Bible. One is the Gihon, and there is a Gihon Hotel in Addis Ababa. It is the Blue Nile and to the east by the Tigris and Euphrates. The Garden of Eden was not a small vegetable garden. It was a vast piece of territory. My own village happens to be just east of the Nile. So I fall in the Garden of Eden. It will surprise many of you that the Prophet Moses was probably married to a Sudanese named Siphorah, as narrated in the book of Numbers.

From the Biblical days, we move to the ancient Sudanese kingdoms of Awach, of Ritat, of Anu, of Maida, that are believed to be connected with the present day Dinka, Shilluk, Nuer, other Nilotic tribes and the peoples of central and western Sudan. At the corridors of history, we move to the Kingdom of Merowe [Arabic Marawi] that bequeathed an iron civilisation to the rest of Africa. Merhawi was transformed into the Christian kingdoms of Nubia. Then followed the spread of Islam and Arab migrations into the Sudan and subsequent collapse of the last Nubian Christian kingdoms of Makuria, Alawa and Soba in 1504, followed by the rise on the etches of the Islamic Kingdom Sinnar, which was founded by the Fuinsh and Shiluk people.

The rest of Sudanese history is familiar to all of us from the Islamic kingdoms of Sinar to the Teko Egyptian occupation, to the first Islamic Mahadisi state, to Anglo-Egyptian condominium to independence in 1956 and the Anyanya movement to 1955 to 1972 to the SPLM/SPLA in 1983, to the second Islamic state in the Sudan of Ingas, with which we negotiated from 1989 and to the comprehensive which we signed today. This is the history of the Sudan, and this is how we got here. It has been a long journey for more than 5,000 years to reach Naivasha and Nyayo Stadium today. It is important to know and appreciate where we came from so we are able to chart clearly the way forward with the momentum of historical force. That was Sudan in history.

Chapter 17

National unity through pluralism and democracy

As for the contemporary Sudan, we have more than 500 different ethnic groups speaking more than 130 different languages. We have two major religions in the country - Islam and Christianity, and traditional African religious. Our contention in the SPLM/SPLA is that the Sudan belongs equally to all the peoples that now inhabit the country and its history, its diversity and richness is the common heritage of all Sudanese. The comprehensive peace agreement that we have signed today is based on this historical and contemporary objective reality of Sudan. By implementing the provisions of the comprehensive peace agreement that we signed today, we (?evolve/emerge) an all-inclusive form of governance that ensures that all Sudanese are equal stakeholders irrespective of where they come from, and this is what will keep our country together.

Furthermore, by adapting and applying the form of governance and wealth-sharing arrangements stipulated in the comprehensive peace agreement to other parts of the country with similar afflictions as the south such as Darfur, eastern Sudan and other parts of the country, we can once again become a great nation that is voluntarily united in diversity rather than divided by diversity and forcibly kept under a coerced and fake unity.

This is the context and the value of the comprehensive peace agreement we have signed today. It provides the Sudan with a real and perhaps the last opportunity to make a real paradigm shift from the old Sudan of exclusivity to the new Sudan of inclusive achieved not through force but through the exercise of the right of self-determination.

Viewed this way the right of self-determination, which is one of the cornerstones of the comprehensive peace agreement, is a blessing rather than a curse as much northern Sudanese fear. I want to assure you that we will all work together with the National Congress Party and other political forces in the Sudan so that we develop a new paradigm so that we keep our country together.

Excellences, distinguished guests, compatriots, ladies and gentlemen, bear with me. I am almost finished. The transformation which shall be engendered by this agreement, which I have alluded to shall be reflected first and foremost in democratic (? mutation) and to which the SPLM is fully committed. Surely by democratic, we do not mean a return to the sham procedural democracy of the past, which was a camouflage for the perpetuation of vested interest. In that sham democracy, civil rights were subject to the whims of rulers. Most Sudanese regions remained peripheral to the central power and were treated as an expendable quantum only to be manipulated through political trickery and double-dealing.

The transformation envisaged in the comprehensive peace agreement puts an end to all that since it represents a political and socioeconomic paradigm shift, which entails the recognition of political diversity by guaranteeing full freedom of political pluralism. The entrenchment of human rights and peoples' rights in the constitution, the upholding of the independence of the judiciary, including the creation of an inviolable constitutional court and commitment to the rule of law by the government and the governed, and the establishment of a truly independent and competent civil service at all levels of government. It also conceptualises and seeks to realise a recreation of the legislature in a manner that shall ensure rigorous checks and balances and guarantees powers to the government of southern Sudan and to the states powers which can neither be withdrawn nor impaired by other centres of power.

Eventually, the comprehensive peace agreement ordains that within a maximum of three to four years governance at all levels shall be mandated by the supreme will of the people through internationally monitored free and fair elections.

Chapter 18

Economic and Social Development

Excellences, distinguished guests, compatriots, ladies and gentlemen, the long war to which we have put an end to today impoverished our citizens and reduced our country with tremendous resources to destitution. Without claiming that the new economic paradigm shift, which I have alluded to, is the ultimate panacea for curing the nation's ills, it provides at least a vision and modalities to address the problems besetting the nation in the here and now - while I leave the world hereafter to those who claim to have divine qualifications.

In southern Sudan and other war-affected areas, as well as in the slums of our major cities, the baseline from which we shall start development is shocking and I will not bore you here with the statistics of the status of these parameters such as prevalence of child malnutrition, primary education, mortality rates among children, rate of maternal mortality, rate of births attended skilled health staff, access to improved water sources. These statistics in southern Sudan and other war-affected areas are among the worst in the world. To combat this pervasive and humiliating poverty and political disenfranchisement, a general policy framework has chartered out and published in a booklet entitled SPLM Strategic Framework for War to Peace Transitions.

In summary, the SPLM shall articulate and implement a social, political and economic development strategy and programmes that include the following highlights:

1. The SPLM shall adopt an economic development paradigm that emphasises growth through rural development and transformation of traditional agriculture that is integrated with agro-industries. We must transform the present subsistence traditional agriculture in southern Sudan and other areas through technological innovations, making agriculture the engine of growth. Agriculture as the engine of growth will literally be fuelled by oil - the building of dikes for flood control and canals and underground water development for irrigation will be priorities to guaranteeing crop production.

2. The SPLM will change the urban-based and centre of focus development paradigm in favour of rural and decentralised development. The SPLM vision, policy and slogan shall be to take the towns of people in the countryside rather than people to towns, where they end up in slums as happened in many countries with the consequent deterioration in their quality of life. Rural small-town planning and rural electrification will, therefore, be priorities.

3. The SPLM shall emphasise and develop new ways of delivery of social services. As we move into the new era of peace, the people of Sudan, particularly the war-affected communities, face formidable social and economic problems and tremendous opportunities. The major problems there require immediate attention fall in the areas of health, education and water. We must find new ways to rapidly and efficiently deliver these services. For example, constructing windmills all over rural Sudan to provide clean drinking water and build micro-dams for generating small-scale hydro-electric power for rural towns as well as the use of solar, wind and biogas energy sources.

4. The SPLM shall exert all efforts to build physical infrastructure - roads, rail and river transport and telecommunications. There

Chapter 18 Economic and Social Development

has never been any tarmac road in the new Sudan since creation, since the days of Adam and Eve, and this is an area the size of Kenya, Uganda, Rwanda and Burundi put together. The SPLM's vision for transport infrastructure is at three levels - to develop regional linkages within southern Sudan and with the neighbours and with northern Sudan and to involve the state and local communities in this infrastructure building.

5. In terms of social and cultural parameters, the SPLM shall adopt the strategies and programmes that shall restore and achieve the dignity of people of the Sudan through social and cultural empowerment. Programmes will include information and media, radio, TV, print, promotion of new Sudan art, songs, dances, theatre of new Sudan, sports, development of local languages and cultures by the various communities of the Sudan, archives of the struggle and modern history of Sudan, archaeology, antiquities and ancient history of Sudan, Africa and the Middle East so that we can find our rightful place in the world.

Chapter 19

Building National Consensus

Excellencies, distinguished guests, ladies and gentlemen, to conclude, the comprehensive peace agreement and safeguards, full compliance with the requirements of the agreement, the SPLM will work in partnership with the National Congress Party. The objectives of this partnership are to ensure a sincere implementation of the comprehensive peace agreement in both letter and spirit and to provide, within the parameters of this agreement, permanent solutions to the problems inherent in Sudan's cultural, social and political diversity.

Failure to appreciate the wealth in diversity was another cause of the national crisis. For diversity, viewed positively is a mutually [word indistinct] phenomenon and ultimately a source of national cohesion and strength. Viewed otherwise, that is a source of dissimilarity or distinction, it shall lead inevitably to the ultimate disintegration of the country as threatens today and which at all costs we must avoid.

Furthermore, the partnership does not mean the abandonment of political allies by any of the two parties. However, this partnership, once safeguarded in the new political dispensation, shall in effect nurture the democratic transformation and political multiplicity, which by their very nature may lead to diverse alliances. But so long as those alliances are based on a commitment to the letter and spirit of the peace agreements that will put an end to the longest war in Africa, alliances become assets not liabilities. It is our submission that political struggle in the Sudan shall henceforth translate into competing visions of peace, progress and development and never into the use of force or the threat of the use of force.

The SPLM, ladies and gentlemen, will ensure that the new political dispensation is wide enough to accommodate all legitimate political and social forces in the country. It is, therefore, our hope to achieve popular consensus on those agreements. As the movement that has been fighting against the marginalisation of others, we shall not tolerate the exclusion of anybody from this process. The parties to the comprehensive peace agreement share this conviction, and we have included in the agreement inclusiveness. In this regard, the SPLM will play its role at the national level to work with the National Congress Party and other political forces to ensure full inclusiveness.

While the SPLM and the National Congress Party shall be major partners in the initial interim government unity, our understanding of partnership is well rooted in inclusiveness, which means to bring on board all political forces in the Sudan, chief among them the political parties within the National Congress Party umbrella and the political parties within the National Democratic Alliance, which we call upon to complete negotiations with the government of Sudan based on the Jeddah agreement that are holding negotiations in Cairo and so that they get their share in the government of national unity and participate and participate fully in all the national commissions stipulated in the comprehensive peace agreement, especially the national constitution review commission.

Finally, on issues that concern southern Sudanese, I want to say a little on south-south dialogue. On building national consensus, the SPLM will also spearhead the south-south dialogue. This dialogue, above all, is to heal wounds and restore fraternity and mutual respect to create a healthier political environment that is accommodative all southern Sudanese political forces, both at the level of southern Sudan and at the national level. But the south-south dialogue is not only about power. It is about democratic exercise based on mature and selfless political discourse among southern Sudanese with a view of galvanising all our human material resources for the service of our people.

Democracy, whether in the north or south, should no longer and solely be a struggle for power but rather as a competition on providing good governance, development and delivering social services for our people and restoring the dignity and wealth of every man and woman. Yet in terms of power-sharing in southern Sudan, I want to assure all that there will be enough room for everybody, including those who have not been associated with the SPLM/SPLA. Even those who for one reason or another were opposed or against the SPLM, there will be a room for everybody.

I want in conclusion to quote, in terms of this inclusiveness, the gospel according to St John that says in St John Chapter 14, Verse 1 and 2: Do not be worried and upset, Jesus told them, believe in God and believe also in me. There are many rooms in my father's house, and I'm going to prepare a place for you. I would not say if it were not true. I say to all southern Sudanese on the occasion of this signing of this comprehensive peace agreement, that there will be many rooms in an SPLM-based government in southern Sudan and all are welcome.

I also want to assure southern Sudanese in general that the comprehensive peace agreement will not be dishonoured like other agreements that Able Aliao [phonetic] has written a book about entitled: Too Many Agreements Dishonoured. The biggest challenge will be the implementation of the peace agreement but we, both the SPLM and the National Congress Party, are committed and fully committed to the implementation of this agreement. There are both external and internal guarantees, organic and external guarantees that will ensure the implementation of this agreement.

I want also to assure the SPLA that the experience of Anyanya I will not repeat itself because there are many SPLA soldiers that are worried they will be left in peace. This regards the issue of funding of the armed forces. We solved the issue of funding of the armed adequately. The joint integrated units, a component of the SPLA, shall be funded by the government of national unity, not as a separate army from the mother SPLM but as part and parcel of it with the same wage and living conditions.

The mother SPLA, on the other hand, will be funded by the government of southern Sudan and the government of southern Sudan has been empowered by the comprehensive peace agreement to raise financial resources from both local and foreign sources and to seek international assistance for that purpose. There is no reason for concern or alarm.

As for those who in the Diaspora, I would like to address them and assure them that the government of southern Sudan, as well as the government of national unity, will their skills, and I take the opportunity of this forum to appeal to all our Diaspora to return home and build our country. As I said before our house has many rooms and Diaspora are welcome to return home and fully participate in the development of southern Sudan, the two areas - Abiey and the whole of Sudan.

Chapter 20

Tributes and Acknowledgements

Finally, I would like to pay tribute to our fallen heroes and martyrs who sacrificed in order for us celebrate this day on both sides of the conflict. Those ladies and gentlemen are the objectives for whose achievements I have exerted all my faculties and energies and efforts, and for which we will cooperate and work together with the National Congress Party. We move in a new direction and achieve the cohesion and the unity of our people and the unity of our country.

Finally, let me pay tribute and salute the courage of the party to reach this agreement and in particular President Umar Hasan al-Bashir and Ustadh Ali Uthman Taha, with whom I sat for 16 months and negotiated this agreement. I salute and congratulate them. I also congratulate the two delegations of the SPLM and the government of Sudan and of course Gen Sumbeiywo and before him Ambassador Daniel Mboya, who was the special envoy, also before them, Zachary Onyango, Bethwel Kiplagat, and foreign minister then Stephen Kalonzo Musyoka and now Minister [for Regional Cooperation John] Koech and other ministers in the Kenya government, who have contributed so much; and to the IGAD [Inter Governmental Authority on Development] envoys of the five countries of IGAD, the facilitators of IGAD, the secretariat. I thank them and congratulate them for guiding the peace process to this successful conclusion.

I would also like to thank and commend the IGAD heads of state, ministers, and peace envoys and indeed the populace who have been with us through thick and thin, guiding, advising, cajoling and sometimes threatening to abandon the process. They deserve praise. Our thanks go to them and also to the bravery of the people of east Africa, the Horn, the Arab world and the wider international community, who on numerous occasions either volunteered to bring peace to Sudan or did encourage in meaningful manners the ongoing peace process. In this connection, the Nigerian efforts of Abuja I and Abuja II, the joint Egyptian-Libyan initiative, the African Union and the Arab League efforts, who exerted efforts for post-conflict reconstruction?

I must also mention a few of the very many names to thank for their contribution to the Sudan peace process, among them are eminent people like President Obasanjo, President Babangida of Nigeria, President Kaunda, Masire, Machel, Nujoma, Chissano, Rawlings, who is here with us today, Mandela of South Africa, Mubarak of Egypt, Qadhafi, Bouteflika, who is here with us today, Jimmy Carter, the late James Grant, and OLS, that has saved millions of lives since 1989, President Bush and his Secretary of State Colin Powell and his special envoy Senator Danforth and Andrew Natsos of USAID, both houses of the US Congress, Prime Minister Tony Blair and his envoys, ambassadors Allan Gulty and McFell, the UN secretary-general and his envoys, ambassadors Sahnun and Pronk, who are here, and a special friend of the Sudan peace process, the Norwegian Minister Hilder Johnson and finally, last but not least, the leaders of this region, led by then President Daniel Arap Moi and now by President Mwai Kibaki, President Museveni, [Ethiopian] Prime Minister [Meles] Zenati, [Eritrean] President [Isayas] Afewerki and the wananchi [citizens] of Kenya and east Africa mzima [as a whole].

Chapter 20   Tributes and Acknowledgements

Finally, I pay tribute and thanks to my dear wife Rebecca and the wives of all my colleagues and comrades in the struggle for their patience and contributions, for without their help the bush would not have been bearable. My sincere thanks to all these people. I pay tribute finally to all the Sudanese people, to whom this peace belongs and I say to them, and I say to them mobruk ol lekum [congratulations]."

It was indeed an amazing speech. As he finished foreigners were so tied, but we as South Sudanese people felt jubilation after John Garang's speech because he could touch our hearts, identify our problems and outline with clarity, our way forward.

After three weeks, I went to the Australia Embassy in Egypt to see how my application was progressing. I was surprised by an officer when she said, 'Congratulations sir, you have been granted a Visa to go to Perth in Western Australia.'

'Oh my god! Thank you so much,' I said. I took the visa and ran home to celebrate with my sister.

That night I didn't sleep at all because my mind was completely occupied by going to Australia. I started to dream big, and I felt that my bad luck and misfortunate were about to vanish immediately I reached Australia. My brother in law (Garang Keynang) helped me enormously when he spoke to Mr Den Jok, who would assist with money to buy my ticket, and then I would repay that as soon as I arrived in Australia. Arrangements took only a short time. I would leave Egypt on 18 February 2005.

One day before I left, my sister Achi Atak Ken organised a farewell party. She invited all the pastors and Aweil community members, especially the elders. They advised me on how to live in Australia by keeping hold of my identity while in Australia. They told me that Australia is a land of opportunity and there would be no doubt of my succeeding, providing I do not misbehave, (otherwise I may not ever be able to return home).

The pastors and local priests prayed for my safe arrival in Australia. Everyone wished me a safe journey including my brother, Athain Mapher, by phone.

On my departure day, I woke up early and got ready to leave. We caught a taxi to the Egyptian International airport. I gave a big thank you to my sister and her family for all their help. I was scared, but I was happy at the same time because I was living my dream. At last, I was on my way to the incredible land Australia. First stop was Singapore.

Inside the plane, the most beautiful girls I ever saw served us. All drinks and different types of food were served.

Due to my lack of English speaking, I was unsure of what to order, so I chose fish and apple – not because I like them, but because these were the only words I knew. Unfortunate. So, every time the flight attendant ladies asked what food and drink I liked?...Fish and apple, I replied. The scenario continued until I reached my first destination, Singapore. There I struggled to find my gate for the next plane. Luckily the three hour stop-over provided plenty of time, and I thanked God I found someone who spoke Arabic who helped me out.

Again, I kept eating and drinking the same food and drink on my way to Western Australia. As we approached Perth International Airport, all passengers were given an arrival form to fill out. I failed to complete the arrival form due to my lack of English. At the airport, the staff tried hard to help me. Finally the staff located an interpreter, over the phone.

Mr Deng Jok had not yet arrived to pick me up because he'd been waylaid at work, but a little later he came with Mr Isaac Luach Luach. On our way to Balga where Deng Jok's home was located Mr Isaac Luach Luach introduced himself more formally and told me that he was a fellow Aweilian. He had arrived here a long time ago through Kenya in east Africa.

'Welcome to your second home brother,' Isaac said.

Chapter 20 Tributes and Acknowledgements

'No worries,' I said.

At home Mr Deng Jok introduced me to his wonderful family – his lovely wife Regina Alek and beautiful children. 'Alek this is Garang Keynang's brother in law,' and he called me Deng Atak Ken. 'Kids, please come and say hello to your uncle who has come from Egypt and he will be here with us for a while until he finds accommodation for himself.'

His children chatted with me. They were so impressed and entertained me with their talk and laughter. They were so cute and funny. They made my first day in Australia a good day.

While I was busy talking with the kids, Deng showed me my living room. At the same time, his wife prepared a very nice lunch for us. As soon I changed my clothes and had a shower I joined everyone in the dining room. But I was so exhausted, I didn't eat much even though it was lovely food. That night I was visited by members of the local Aweil community; the Chairman of the WA Aweil Community Association, the late David Kier. They all welcomed me and wished me well.

Two days later, I called both Achai's family and my other Khartoum family, including my mother. They were happy and grateful to hear my voice and that I was safe.

At Deng Jok's house and the homes of other fellow-Aweilians I started to see the goodness of Australia. Deng also took me to Centrelink to arrange my social welfare. Three weeks later I found work in a Farm Factory Company. I was able to send some money to my mother and the rest of the Atak Ken's family back home. Often, I supported my Sister Achai Atak. I worked in that company for one month only, and cleared my debt for my ticket with Den Jok.

Three months later I enrolled in Certificate 1 in reading and writing English in Victoria TAFE in Perth city. Although I had finished my secondary schooling in Arabic, my level of English was poor. It was part of 510 hours that the Australian

Government offers to the new arrivals especially those who are struggling with English. Every morning I took the bus and joined a lot of migrant people who were in the same situation as myself. I struggled in even basic aspects of the language like buying food, attending to my personal needs like buying a ticket or having a little conversation in English with Australian people. I felt shy and embarrassed. I even ran away from Australian people if they were trying to speak to me. But English seemed a difficult language to me. I tried to do whatever I could and stay calm and be positive no matter what.

I studied full time with great curiosity and determination to learn to speak and write as well as possible. I worked very hard to get over my embarrassment and to integrate into Australian society. I found TAFE helpful but the teaching system is completely different.

In Sudan, the teachers do their best to give students 25% of the information and the rest is for the student to do. In contrast, Australian teachers just give less than 5% of the information and the rest is up to the student. Therefore, it was a big challenge for beginners and anyone struggling like me who has no Basic English skills at all and no clue about working with a computer. In addition, there was no class competition like the one we had back home, so everyone has to work hard and tirelessly for himself in order to pass the class.

During that period, I experienced a terrible cough. My local doctor failed to diagnose any specific disease. But the Royal Perth clinic diagnosed TB. They told me not to worry about it. They gave me a strong medication to take for 6 months, then I slowly started to get better.

On July 30, 2005, the world was shocked at the report of the death of the First Vice President of Sudan and President of Southern Sudan, Dr John Garang. The South Sudanese people around the world were especially dismayed when they heard the report that he had died in a helicopter crash. It was blamed on pilot error.

We couldn't believe that we had lost our champion, John Garang. He gave all for us. On numerous occasions, he proved that he was there for us, for the vulnerable ones. A lot of us lost hope that there would never be another one like.him. My uncle Agany Agany ken in Khartoum told me, 'Everything is finished now because no one is going to be there for us.'

But I told him to take courage because the same God who provided Garang for us, will provide someone else. There was chaos and turmoil in the Sudan capital. A lot of lives were lost and properties destroyed in Khartoum. There was panic.

In Australia, as a sign of mourning, South Sudanese people did not go to work or school. Some cried in public places.

Why did this happen? Who was behind it? What will happen to the Comprehensive peace agreement? General Salva Kiir Mayardit became the new leader of the SPLM/ SPLA. Therefore, he will be first Vice President of Sudan and President of South Sudan.

The international body, the African union, the IGAD and the President of the Sudan, Omar Hassan Al-Bashir, confirmed to the Sudanese and Southerners not to lose hope because of the death of Dr John Garang; that it will not bring an end to the Peace Agreement, no matter what. President Bashir emphasised that the peace belongs to the Sudanese people.

A year later I moved away from Deng Jok's house to a new property in Thorney Way in Balga, where I joined both Mr Garang Deng Akol and Bol Garang Akon. Together we could pay the rent and support each other emotionally and financially.

Before I left Deng's house, I gave a big thank you to Deng Jok and his family for all their help and support that they gave me. It meant a lot to me. In my new home, I could get my 'L' plates for my driving license, my learner's provisional license. Mr Martin Milit Deng helped me to pass the test. Later I got my full license and thanked almighty God who helped me to conquer that test. In the same year, I finished my Certificate 2 in reading and writing English with distinction! Then I enrolled in Tuart College when my 510 hours English training had finished. After I passed their complicated entry tests, I enrolled at Tuart College in Certificate 2 general education for Adults.

Furthermore, every Sunday morning since 2005 I offered myself voluntarily and served in the St. Bakhita Catholic Church as a liturgical organiser and chorister. It is mainly a South Sudanese Church where we use both Arabic and English.

Father Sam, from India, is in charge and speaks both languages eloquently. He is a very good priest. For example, he told us a very interesting and funny story about love and forgiveness:

'There was a priest in one of the churches who was talking about forgiving our enemies and neighbours. He preached for about 15 minutes, then asked the believers, 'How many of you will forgive your enemies and neighbours?'

Fifty per cent of the people raised their hands. He continued preaching for another 15 minutes and asked the same question, for a second time. This time about eighty per cent of the people raised their hands. But the priest was still not happy, so he preached for another 15 minutes and asked for a third time, 'How many of you will forgive your enemies and neighbours?'

This time, the congregation realised that the priest would not let them go and might preach all day long. They all raised their hands, except for one old lady. He asked her, 'Please come forward and explain to us why you don't want to forgive your enemies Ma'am.

The old lady responded, 'Father, look at me. I'm 94 years old and all my enemies have gone a long time ago!'

Chapter 20 Tributes and Acknowledgements

At home, we had meaningful and very useful social gatherings with relatives, colleagues and friends who joined us every weekend. Some came from south of the river. Others joined us from Mandurah, which is about 75 kilometres away from Balga. During those meetings, we encouraged and supported each other financially. We discussed various ideas that everyone could benefit from. It was like a counselling place and it would relieve stress. If you were discouraged, you would find someone to encourage you and make you feel better. Some brought sophisticated or complicated issues to the group, and through open discussion, people could find a solution. It was a good place to be that we all benefitted from it. Plus, it was a tremendous social atmosphere!

The people who would visit us were:

Martin Garan Aher

Deng Den Mou

Isaac Luach Luach

Adupt Aguer Nogr

Garang Yout Yout

Garang Tong Kon

Thiik Deng Riiny

Milit Makuag Koul

Chan Aweech Jongkor

Ustaz Ayel Baak

Malou Kuach

Areil

However, every time I had a chance, I would work to support myself financially. I worked in places such as: Danish

Patisserie, Staff Link, Batter Enterprise, City of One Wanneroo and Goodman Fielder. In 2008.

I had a severe accident at the Mirrabooka traffic lights. Thank God, I was safe, but my car was damaged for good. After an investigation, I was found guilty. Therefore, I had to pay for the other guy's car to be fixed. It was a difficult moment, but with God's grace, I could arrange the repairs, and bought a new car for myself.

In July 2009, I enrolled in the Certificate 2 program in Surveying (Mining & Engineering) at central TAFE. I committed to that intensive course after I finished my Certificate 2 in General Education. Regrettably, a few weeks later I found that it was the wrong course for me, because I did not have a passion for the subject of mining. It was a big challenge for somebody like me to find what I love and what I want to be in the future. I can pass any course, yet still not have a passion for it. Having said that, in July 2009 I did pass the mining course and enrolled in a different course called Certificate 3 in Accounting. During that class, I struggled a lot because it was boring and I just didn't like it. However, I used it as a tool to get me into the University. Who knows maybe I will find something interesting enough for me. That same year, I served as an information officer at Mading Aweil Community Association in WA under the leadership of Isaac Luach Luach. I was a very active member and entertained a lot of Aweil members. I proved to the whole community that I am strong and shine when thing gets tough. They knew me, and I knew them all. I considered some of them as my role models. I also listened to our elders all the time because some of them are brilliant and they did illuminate my future.

During that time, Isaac's team did an outstanding job offering a lot of help and assistance to our community. Before Isaac became chairman of our community, he helped many members, myself included. For example, Isaac helped a lot of people find accommodation. He was one of few who had a full license and his own transport at that time. He was a generous and talented young man who always wanted to help his fellow Aweilians, especially those in need. He gave his time and left his other commitments to go to those who didn't speak English very well in government departments and hospitals. Our community owes Isaac a big 'thank you' for a tremendous job well done. Moreover, in the same year, I could pass Certificate 3 in Accounting and was awarded my certificate.

It was a good year for me because another of my dreams also became a reality when I received my Australian citizenship on 16 September 2009, after I passed the citizenship test. I received my citizenship in a big ceremony, which was attended by more than 75 people. It was an unforgettable moment when I held the certificate in my hand. I had been granted the title and became a full Aussie during the Australian Citizenship ceremony. We were told that 'becoming an Australia citizen means you call Australia home, with both privileges and responsibilities.' It was a meaningful and wonderful occasion. I was able to say to myself that I'm Australian (Aussie), even though I wasn't born here, and was amazed at how lucky I am to have that important privilege. I am proud to be now an Australian.

At the ceremony, I was emotionally moved when we sang the Australian National Anthem:

Australians all let us rejoice,
For we are young and free;
We've golden soil and wealth for toil;
Our home is girt by sea;
Our land abounds in nature's gifts;
Of beauty rich and rare;
In history's page, let every stage
Advance Australia Fair
In joyful strains then let us sing,
Advance Australia Fair.

Beneath our radiant Southern Cross,
We'll toil with hearts and hands,
To make this Commonwealth of ours
Renowned of all the lands,
For those who've come across the seas
We've boundless plains to share,
With courage, let us all combine
To advance Australia fair.
In joyful strains then let us sing,
Advance Australia fair.

It was a fantastic national anthem with its touching words! At the end, we were invited for hot drinks and biscuits. I returned home happy. Yes, it was a magnificent and incredible day!

Since my arrival in Western Australia (WA), I have visited many states, such as Victoria, New South Wales and South Australia. I have friends and relatives in these areas. The eastern states are beautiful and astonishing, but I like my home state most.

While living in WA, I found a real friend, by the name of Thiik Deng Riiny, who helped me a lot. I consider him not only a friend but a brother whom I found in diaspora, where it is very difficult to find someone to stand beside you in hardship and difficult moments.

Mr Henri. J. M. Nouwen once said: 'When we honestly ask ourselves which person in our lives means the most to us, we often find that it is those who, instead of giving advice, solutions, or cures, have chosen to rather share our pain and touch our wounds with a warm and tender hand. The friend who can be silent with us in a moment of despair or confusion, who can stay with us in an hour of grief and bereavement, who can tolerate not knowing, not curing, not healing and face with us the reality of our powerlessness. That is a friend who cares.'

Chapter 20 Tributes and Acknowledgements

My friend, Thiik Deng Riiny and his lovely wife did a lot for me. I thank them from the bottom of my heart for their support and encouragement in times of need.

It would be a huge mistake not to mention other people in my book, such as Elizabeth Sama Moyeen and her husband, who gave me enormous support. She helped me a lot financially and emotionally. Elizabeth is well known in our community as my mother in Australia, due to her strong support and strong commitment to stand with me in the good and difficult moments. When she went to South Sudan, she visited my real mother, Abuk Mayol Amoi. Elizabeth is a strong woman in our WA community and highly respected.

In January 2011, I participated in the South Sudan Referendum after our SPLM chapter in WA (at that time under the leadership of Mr Khamis Tombe) brought the ballot box to WA, for South Sudanese people to participate in that historic event. That referendum was done to comply with what had been signed in 2005, in Naivasha, between SPLM and the Khartoum Central Government.

The referendum was about whether South Sudan should remain a part of whole Sudan or become an independent nation. I voted in favour of the separation of the South, due to the deep mistrust that had been created among our people over the past few decades, which would make it very difficult for us to live as one nation again. I voted for separation of the South because I don't want to be a second-class citizen in my own country. As Dr John Garang illustrated clearly when he said, 'I and those who joined me in the bush and fought for more than 20 years have brought to you CPA on a golden plate. Our mission is accomplished. It is now your turn, especially those who did not have a chance to experience bush life. When the time comes to vote on the referendum, it will be your golden chance to determine your fate. Would you like to vote to be second-class citizens in your own country? It is absolutely your choice.'

In 2010, I completed both the Certificate 4 in Accounting and Diploma of Accounting, at West Coast Institute of Training before I engaged myself in the referendum process. I completed both qualifications in the unprecedented and most difficult moment I had witnessed in my life so far. That period was a bit harder and more challenging, which meant I did not take them for granted at all. First, I was surprised and shocked when Mr Garang Deng Akol left us and decided to look elsewhere for new accommodation.

Consequently, Bol Garang and I ended up paying the rent of $6oo AUD every fortnight by ourselves. That was okay for Mr Bol because at that time he was working. But for me, it was a nightmare because I was a full-time student! Knowingly, I got $480 AUD, as Newstart Allowance every two weeks from Centrelink. But this money was nothing compared to the financial situation I was in. I had to pay $300 AUD to the owner of the property as part of the rent payment. Then, I ended up with only $150 AUD, which made it very hard for me if I wanted to buy accounting books, pay school fees every semester, and pay the bills every three months. I was dying financially.

It was a big challenge for me just to buy food. Sometimes, I would sleep without food and go to school without a lunch box or even $5 in my pocket to buy chips and a sandwich. To make the matter worse, I found it very difficult to tell friends and colleagues about it. As the situation continued, I realised that even in rich mighty Australia you could taste hunger and starvation if you didn't pay attention. I missed my mother, because if she was here, she wouldn't let me face this situation alone, and I wouldn't be starving like this I thought.

Even in starving Sudan with its difficult circumstances, my mother could feed us. I had never felt as hungry the way I felt when I was in Thornley Way in Balga, WA. This situation remained for a while. Every day I had to go to the shop to buy cheap foods such as eggs, breakfast and biscuits. Even though money is not everything, it is indeed embarrassing when the money isn't there!

However, my miserable situation and severe financial status was alleviated when I was given accommodation by Foundation Housing, which is government housing, where I paid rent according to what I earned each fortnight.

The new home was in the same area. I also looked for work so that I could visit my family home and get married as soon as possible. Some weeks later I was employed by Integrated in a labour position. There, I found a talkative Australian boy who asked me some challenging questions. He asked, 'Deng, how long have you been in Australia?'

'Almost five years, sir,' I replied.

'Do you like it?' he asked.

'Well, your question is a bit wide, but Australia is overwhelmingly fantastic, even though some of its aspects aren't easy for me,' I said. 'Brother, there is no place like home.'

However, at that time I was in contact with Athain and my mother, and they were asking me to visit them at home. I promised I would, before the end of 2011. On 9th July 2011, we celebrated our independence day with joy and jubilation, particularly we as South Sudanese people in Perth, Western Australia. All tribes gathered in the Mirrabooka recreation centre and congratulated themselves for a job well done! Those who were too emotional started to cry tears of happiness and joy – it was like a dream for them. Some were dancing and thanked God for his great help. Young men, myself included, started to dream bigger. I was dreaming for a great, peaceful and prosperous South Sudan to pay back for all those suffering and misfortunate periods we had all been through. But unfortunately, in years to come I would be proven wrong.

Back home, huge numbers of South Sudanese danced with exhilaration in the capital, Juba, as our new country formally declared its independence, a hard-won separation from the north. It was an unforgettable moment for the sons and daughters of South Sudan. It was history-making. How lucky we were to witness such a remarkable and historic event. Many had fought long and hard for this day to arrive.

These were some wonderful pictures that were captured on that wonderful day.

Chapter 20 Tributes and Acknowledgements

For the first time ever we could sing our own national anthem with pride and dignity knowing we are the owners of that beautiful land, which God has chosen for us with His blessing and unlimited bounties.

Deng Atak Ken

The national anthem of South Sudan is as follows:

Oh God

We praise and glorify you

For Your grace on South Sudan,

The land of great abundance

Uphold us united in peace and harmony.

Oh motherland

We rise raising flag with the guiding star

And sing songs of freedom with joy;

For justice, liberty and prosperity

Shall forever more reign?

Oh, great patriots

Let us stand up in silence and respect,

Saluting our martyrs whose blood

Cemented our national foundation,

We vow to protect our nation.

Oh God, bless South Sudan.

Chapter 21

My Journey back to South Sudan after more than 22 years

Some months after the independence of South Sudan, I helped my family financially and took them back to their home, after South Sudan became a safe, secure and good place for everyone to live. Their arrival was confirmed to me by my brother, Athain Atak. They were delighted to return to Aweil town. I talked to my mother on the phone, and she expressed her happiness and satisfaction with what South Sudan looked like. She invited me to come and visit, to view the situation for myself. I promised I would. Without further ado, I went straight away to the Commonwealth Bank and applied for a loan of $15,000 and made a promise to pay them back when I returned from my holidays.

Three days later, I got an important call from the Commonwealth Bank, telling me the application was successful, but they needed my presence to finalise the loan. I went there and signed some documents and then the money was transferred to my account immediately.

I then sped up the process to leave. I applied for my passport, and I got it within two weeks. I booked my ticket for departure at the beginning of December, so that I could celebrate the birth of Christ with my relatives and family. The process was easy in Australia, nothing was complicated, unlike my previous country, Sudan.

I informed friends, relatives in WA and my family about my travelling. The day before I left Perth, I organised a little farewell and prayers at home. It was well attended. I thanked everyone for being with me, particularly my second mother in WA, Elizabeth Sama, who did an unbelievable job that day. From the bottom of my heart, I thanked her so much for her sacrifices, diligence and fatigue during that small gathering. She contributed physically and financially and made that farewell meaningful. Without her, I wasn't sure how I would have managed.

I left Perth International Airport for the Thailand International Airport. This time I was confident and able to select different foods and drinks the way I liked because my English had significantly improved, and I could communicate perfectly. With that said, I was about to get a girlfriend within the flight attendant girls because they were so impressed with my English. At 2.00 pm the next day, I arrived at Juba international Airport, after I passed through Addis Abba.

At Juba International Airport, I was received by Mr Gorgy Agany, Mr Kout Agany and my little brother Agany Atak. From there, they took me home where they lived. Then I called my mother in Aweil to confirm my arrival. I received welcoming calls from many people, including my half-brother Mr Athain Atak Ken. I told everyone it was very nice to be back home.

That night, I could not sleep because I kept receiving calls from people who knew me personally, inside and outside of Juba.

In the morning, my brother Agany Atak took me to the Juba market so I could view the city because I had never been to that area in my entire life. I caught up with so many friends and relatives. We took many pictures together and had fun. It was

Chapter 21 My Journey back to South Sudan after more than 22 years

a good time for me, even though Juba city is overcrowded. I had been in the capital of the Republic of South Sudan for two weeks. I tried to get a flight to take me home, to Aweil City, but unfortunately, all my attempts were unsuccessful, due to the lack of flights. Christmas was a busy time for travelling. Therefore, I ended up with no option but to get the bus to Wau, and then to Aweil Town. On 20 December, my brother Agany and I left the Juba bus station by bus.

It was a very interesting journey, despite difficulties we faced on the way. The road was very bad, so when we reached Wau we were tired, fatigued and exhausted due to the long distance. When I arrived, I immediately threw away the clothes I was wearing that day because they were full of desert dust.

When we reached Rumbek city the driver stopped for all to have lunch. My brother and I had bought some sandwiches. While we had our lunch, a disabled man approached me and said, 'We fought for more than two decades in the bush for you guys to be a minister and enjoy it. Is that the case minister, while we are suffering? Do you think that is fair?'

'I'm not a minister, sir,' I told him. But regrettably, he refused to believe me and was so angry, he wanted to fight me. Thank God, at that moment my little brother got involved by telling him to leave or something not good would happen to him.

Agany said, 'This guy is not a minister as you think, and certainly, he is not from here, so please leave us alone.' The man said no more.

I was deeply surprised by that situation, but my brother told me not to be worried. He said, 'You will see this kind of misbehaviour in so many places in South Sudan because there is no justice and things aren't perfect here.'

I asked people when we would reach Wau town. One of the passengers told me it would be 18 hours. Inside the bus it was quiet, but people were listening to South Sudanese music. I was really bored. At 9.00 pm on the same day, we reached Tonj town and our small bus stopped again for us to have dinner before we entered Wau.

At the restaurant, while everyone was busy trying to get something to eat, an old man approached the driver and warned him not to drive fast if he was about to enter Wau because there is a big mountain on that border. When I asked why he could not find a safer road, I was told that there is no other road that can take you to Wau. If you are going to Wau then you must pass through that those mountains because it is the only way. It is a dangerous path because the road is narrow at the top of the mountain and it is easy for a vehicle to lose control, fall and kill people.

The driver told the man, 'No problem. I got it. I know this mountain and how to deal with it very well. I heard last week that one bus drove off that mountain and killed everyone who was on it. Therefore, I have to be vigilant and attentive.'

When I asked why the Government doesn't do something about it, he told me that no-one cares. 'It seems you are not from here, that's why you asked,' he said.

After half an hour, we were back inside the bus again, this time a bit worried. As the bus left Tonj, I started to feel so much worry and anxiety that nothing else occupied my mind, apart from that nightmare mountain I was about to cross over.

I started to pray and asked God to protect us. After three hours, I asked the driver where we were and if we had passed that mountain yet. 'We passed it a long time ago, sir. We are just 15 minutes away from entering Wau,' he responded.

'Oh my god, why you didn't tell me?' I said. 'I was scared and in turmoil, waiting to see that mountain.' The driver simply responded, 'Sorry, but we have passed it.'

Chapter 21 My Journey back to South Sudan after more than 22 years

I was relieved from the pressure and I started to feel good again. At around midnight, we arrived in Wau town safely. My brother and I slept in the hotel because we knew nobody in that zone. In the morning, we took another bus to our hometown, Aweil. It took us only three hours to arrive there, and we took another bus straight away to my village, Arieth, where my relatives, including my mother, lived.

As we arrived at Arieth bus station, we found everyone waiting patiently for our arrival. As soon they saw me, the entire family ran towards me and gave me warm greetings and hugs. I did the same to them, one by one, without excluding any family member. Some people who hadn't heard my name for a long time and hadn't seen me were struggling to recognise me. I didn't know them in person either. Some family members were joyfully crying. It was a wonderful emotional reunion. At that time, people were talking about nothing but my arrival. They made me feel valued by the way they received me. I also made them feel valued because I was the first one to come back from such a prestigious place as mighty Australia.

I began to believe what Michael Fox said about family: 'Family is not an important thing. It's everything.' That was well stated by him! At that time, my mother wasn't there because she was very sick and had decided to wait for me at home. At home, I received a warm welcome from my mother, and she said, 'Deng, my son, I'm so sorry because I was supposed to join the rest of the family who was waiting for your arrival for a long time at the bus station. But, as you can see, in my situation, I couldn't do that.'

I replied, 'Come, Mother, I absolutely understood your situation before you even spoke a single word. For your information, your apology is accepted. There is nothing to worry about. Your sickness will go away now because your loving son is here. I will do everything in my power to make sure you are one hundred per cent healthy. Nothing will bother you at all, as long I'm here, Mother.'

Then she gave me a big hug. 'Your words are powerful, son. I am already starting to get better now. I don't need a doctor anymore because I saw you and heard your beautiful and encouraging words. You make me proud. You are still strong and never changed. You are a magnificent son,' mother said.

That night I didn't sleep because my mother and the rest of the family kept talking to me all night. In the morning, I gave everyone some money as a gift and thanked them for being able to wait for me at the bus station for so long. It was magnificent. Please keep that family unity alive for some challenging times ahead. They said that family is 'like branches on a tree, our lives may grow in different directions yet our roots remain as one.' From the bottom of my heart I thanked everyone. During the days that I spent at home I received calls from relatives and friends within and outside South Sudan, including my half-brother Athain Atak, who called me from time to time and who gave me some advice.

From my part, I didn't call so many people, but I did call Mr Karol Ken Ken, who had done a great job searching for a partner for me.

After Christmas, my mother organised a big welcoming party to give big thank you to Almighty God for bringing me home safely after being absent for a long time. It was an awesome party, and I saw joy and jubilation in everyone's face. Our traditional dances were wonderfully presented. I tried to join them in dance, but my dancing was not so good, even though I was doing my best to imitate them. I'm not good at traditional dances at all. On the other hand, it was well attended by our local politicians and our local police officers. They all were given a chance to speak. They all thanked me for coming back home. In the end, I was given the final opportunity to speak and give those who attended a word of appreciation. People were very happy to see and hear me, and they clapped.

My speech was as follows:

'Our police officers who joined us this evening, representative of Sultan of Atokthou, distinguished guests, my fellow Aweilians, ladies and gentlemen, good evening. My name is Deng Atak Ken, son of this wonderful and well-respected family of my Dad, Atakdit, who fought so hard to establish this family. Actually, I'm coming from the land of opportunity called Australia. I left this staggering and terrific country when I was a little boy, in 1989, when this region was war-torn, and my mother, like many other mothers, ran away to find a better place for us. To find a safer and healthier environment for us. For that, we as Abuk's sons and daughters, in particular, owe her a big thank you, from the bottom of our hearts, for accomplishing her mission successfully.

However, when things got tough in Khartoum, I ran away, alone, into Egypt and from Egypt to where I'm coming from today. But remember, things are happening according to God's will and of course, they are 'happening for a strong reason'.

The country I'm coming from, which is becoming my second home right now, has given me a lot and, from the bottom of my heart, I thank Australia. Indeed, without it I wouldn't be able to be here strong and positive. Australian people are like any other human beings on earth, some are bad and some people are incredible. But overwhelmingly, Australia is a good place to be, and I thank God for putting me there.

In Australia, the life is very easy. But can also be tough and challenging in some ways. If you want to be a bad person, then guess what? You will be. But, if you want to be a successful person that society can rely on, you will fulfil your dreams. As you know, life is all about choices and how you want it to be, and with choices come consequences. That is the beauty of the world we are living in!

My message to you all is to pray a lot, so God can change our leaders' hearts and make them better leaders - not replicate the suffering and mistreatment we witnessed from the oppressive Khartoum Government. If they cannot change the incompetence and misjudgements, then guess what? God will change them peacefully, without a single person getting hurt.

You must abandon and relinquish human jealousy, hatred, selfishness and greed. Otherwise, you won't be able to move forward because they always take the country backwards. The country where I am coming from is united, and the citizens speak with one voice. That's why you can see how peaceful and evolved their nation is, despite the huge differences they have among themselves.

Finally, I thank everyone for coming and leaving all your commitments to join us this beautiful evening. It means a lot to the family, and it means a lot to me personally. May God bless you and your families.

Thank you so much.'

When I ended my talk, they all stood up and gave me a warm and big clap. Some people approached me afterwards and said, 'Your words are meaningful, admirable, powerful and touching. May God bless you.'

On one of the nights, Mr Athain told me to call Mr Karol Ken Ken because he is a good man and he may help me find my partner as soon as possible. It didn't take long for me to do that but, unfortunately, Ken was living in Aweil town which meant I had to travel to town. That time, I was joined by Mr Makuag Tong Agany. We stayed there for some weeks. There, in Aweil, Mr Karol Ken introduced me to many girls, but I didn't like any of them.

Chapter 21 My Journey back to South Sudan after more than 22 years

One day, in an area called Mathiang, Aweil South Sudan, he introduced me to a beautiful girl called Abuk Kuach Ngor, who is not only going to be my sweetheart but my wife. That night, I couldn't stop thinking about her, and her amazing picture remains in memory. Then I talked to the family about it, and I was given a tick to go ahead if I 'love' her. I arranged another meeting with Abuk Kuach, and I personally informed her that I wanted her to be my wife if she didn't mind. Without further ado, she gave me her full consent. I started to put marital relationship traditional procedures in place to make everyone happy, especially Abuk's family.

Having been arranged through the traditional and customary unwritten laws, on 25 February 2012 a dowry of 13 head of cattle was initially given to Abuk's family, which happened after her family gave my family their acceptance and blessing to this marriage.

In the end, both families agreed to organise a wedding day in the future. On that day, Abuk's family would tell us how many cows in total they were looking for. Then we would tell them what we could do. While I was enjoying my new life, my mother's health was deteriorating, so I took her to many hospitals in and around Aweil. Thank God her health started to show some recovery and quick improvement.

However, due to my business, I wasn't able to visit many places in Aweil, which made a lot of families and friends angry with me because I was not able to visit them. However, I made a promise to myself that, if I come back again, I will do my best to make sure I visit them.

Moreover, before I left Aweil and South Sudan, I met some of the people I knew when I was in Khartoum, as well as some of my old friends and classmates. Some of them recognised me and some regrettably didn't. Some people were delighted to see me back home, and they were very humble. Some were too arrogant, and they didn't appreciate me coming back at all.

Some were furious to realise that I came back from a most prestigious country such as Australia, fearing that I would take their position away from them. But I disregarded all these and focused only on my visit. Overwhelmingly, I did enjoy that trip, even though my country still needs much more development. As I said earlier, I didn't visit many places, but the few I saw told me a lot. For example, we lack schools, infrastructure and professional medical people. A very simple disease could kill people, and nothing is available in terms of facilities.

After three months, I left the republic of South Sudan with unforgettable memories and promising my wife to complete the marriage process as soon as possible. As well as pay for the rest of the cattle to her family, according to what both families had agreed upon.

It was an emotional time leaving at Aweil's domestic airport because my wife-to-be and my half-brother's wife, Abuk Diing, were crying to see me leaving them again. But I made it very clear to them that, no matter what, I would come back, in Jesus name.

On 7 March 2012, I was met by my best friend ever, Mr Thiik Deng Riiny, at Perth International Airport. I was more confident and motivated than ever because I felt I had another mission to accomplish in the coming months. I had to find a way to bring my lovely wife to my second home as soon as possible. I would have to find a good job to be able to fulfil that dream. In the airport, I thanked God for giving me a good friend such as Thiik Deng who is always available to help. I was in contrast with the Kenyan parable that says, 'You choose your friends, and God will choose your neighbours,' because I have strong confidence and conviction that it was Almighty God who chose Mr Thiik to be there for me, anytime I felt I needed help.

At home, in Balga, I was astonished by the wonderful welcoming reception that had been organised by Thiik's wife and the Aweil community members, especially those who are so dear to me. It

Chapter 21   My Journey back to South Sudan after more than 22 years

was fantastic. I really appreciated it. It meant a lot to me, and it was great to be back to my second home. That evening, we had a wonderful social gathering.

I was asked so many friendly questions like, 'How did I arrange my marriage?' and 'What were the main obstacles?'

Some friends asked me about their relatives back home. I was able to brief everyone on what exactly took place, and I answered their questions accordingly. Additionally, I offered my humble apologies to everyone whose relatives I didn't visit, due to time limitations.

My phone was also very busy because I was receiving so many calls from those who wanted to welcome me back and congratulate me on my marriage. I also received a phone call from my (intended) wife, to make sure I arrived safely in Western Australia. It was a fantastic day!

In the morning, I went to so many job network agencies looking for work, but unfortunately, I couldn't find a job. Three weeks later, I found a cleaning job at Goodman Fielder through one workforce recruitment agent. It wasn't a good job but I had to take it, due to the circumstance that I was in. I had been doing a magnificent job there, and my boss was so impressed.

In the meantime, I was in contact with my mother, Athain Mapher, and my lovely wife-to-be. During that consistent conversation, I had been asked not to wait until I came back to do my wife's process. With that said, I sent my wife-to-be to the South Sudan capital, Juba, to try to get basic documents for herself, such as a birth certificate (because she told me that she'd lost her birth certificate) as well as nationality and passport documents. With God's help, she could get these.

On the other hand, I was sending too much money to my half-brother, George Agany, to buy cows for my wedding because my in-laws were asking for their rights. Mr Georgy took that seriously because he is well-known as a serious man, and he bought many cows.

However, due to the continuation of my wedding, I had been invited by my in-laws here in Australia to Mr James Jok's house. I went there with friends and relatives. There my in-laws welcomed me to the family and expressed their happiness and gratitude to have somebody like me coming into their family through intermarriage. Especially Mr Malou Kuach, who had previously predicted that I would marry a girl who is related to him in some shape or form. It was an astonishing prediction. I illustrated clearly to the crowd in attendance that I was well blessed.

I got the opportunity to say something to my in-laws concerning their appreciated invitation. 'My in-laws, those who came here with me, Aweil community members, ladies and gentlemen. I'm standing here before you all to acknowledge and confess that Mr Malou Kuach was right in his prediction a long time ago. That's why I'm standing here today, as one of the family. I don't know how it happened, but what God put in Malou's mouth, before I even thought about marriage, is exactly what is taking place.'

I also thanked all the in-laws for their invitation. It meant a lot to me. Lastly, I gave an enormous thank you to those who attended the very nice gathering.

We stayed there for a whole day, and it was unforgettable! When we came back, I informed both mother and Athain of that wonderful invitation, and they said, 'You have started to enjoy your wedding already. Good for you!'

In the same year, I went to the Department of Immigration and paid $2,750 AU for a partner visa. I was furious about such a high payment I had to pay at that moment. I asked the officer why this visa was so expensive. 'I don't know, sir. It used to be less but, in the last few years, it has increased,' she said. She then added, 'it is under the government's responsibility, Sir.'

'I know it is the government, but what is the message they are giving? The government should promote the reunion of families and make things easy for them, not the other way around,' I said.

'I don't know, sir,' she said. In the end, I had no other option but to pay the money to bring my wife in to Australia. It was a condition for our reunion. At the same time, I grabbed the partner form to fill out because it was one of the things required for me to complete.

I wasn't confident to fill in the partner application form so I asked Mr Martin Garang Aher, who is more of an expert, more experienced in that regard, to help me in the matter. Thank God, he agreed to do it straightaway, as he always did. To be honest, I was emotionally moved and touched by the kindness and goodness of Mr Martin Garang Aher, to me and to everyone else in our Community. Since we'd met here in 2006, in our second home, Western Australia, Mr Martin had done a lot for me. He was always there for me when I needed him, like others, and he didn't disappoint if I needed help. Martin was the person I consulted on a regular basis, if I was broken financially and emotionally. He was the person I relied on if things got tough and I didn't know what to do. In other words, he was like my mentor, before he decided to stop doing things for me anymore, due to his business and other issues that I might or might not know. I only hope I didn't do something silly or disturbing in the process.

Mr Martin Garang Aher Arol's assistance to me was unforgettable. The man didn't leave any stone unturned to move me forward as a strong person the community could rely on in the future. He was the guy who helped me open both my Yahoo email account and Facebook account; and he was the one who helped with my computing.

He not only filled out my wife's application form, but he advised me to take my wife to Kenya, where his wonderful mother lives. He also introduced me to his half-brother, Bol Aher, in Nairobi, who did an outstanding job for me and my wife in Kenya by providing all kinds of help. Martin was the one who stood with me, giving me some strong advice when I was so worried and anxious, particularly the time my wife was very sick in Kenya. I thank Mr Martin Garang Aher Arol for what he did for me, I really owe him a big thank you for the exceptional help.

However, even though nothing is ever certain and nothing remains forever, relationships included, Mr Martin should be proud for the help he provided me, and if I become famous tomorrow, I wouldn't forget him. Because I don't have anything specific to reward him or pay him back with, I think it would be an enormous mistake if I missed mentioning the great help I got from him in my book!

If our friendship stops here, or he ceases to help me normally, he should remember one significant thing – no one could 'delete' the help he and his family provided to me and my family. His name will always strongly remain in my memory as the one who helped me most in my transitional period, to be somebody who can run his affairs independently and be able to help others, who might face the same difficulties.

Elizabeth Gilbert once said: 'In the end, though, maybe we must all give up trying to pay back the people in this world who sustain our lives. In the end, maybe it's wiser to surrender before the miraculous scope of human generosity and to just keep saying thank you, forever and sincerely, for as long as we have voices.' In the end, this is exactly what I will do, I will keep saying thank you, Mr Martin Garang Aher, for what you did, whenever I have an opportunity to do just that.

Before I left Perth for the second time, I borrowed more money from the Commonwealth Bank. I did ask for $10,000 AUD, but unfortunately, they only gave me $5,000 AUD. Thank God, I was able to get financial support from the following people:

Mr Adup Aguer Ngor gave me, $300 equivalent to one cattle

Mr Ken Athain gave me, $500 equivalent to two cattle

Mr Chan Aweech Jangkour gave me, $300 equivalent to one cattle

Mr Malith Makuch koul, $300 equivalent to one cattle

Mr Garang yout yout, $100

In Law Kawach Kawach Makuei, $500 equivalent to two cattle

Khon Khon, $300 equivalent to one cattle

Marenk Makoi, $300 equivalent to one cattle

Santino Akoi, $50 USA

Garang Dut Ngong, $300 equivalent to one cattle

Garang Dut's wife, Abuk Baak $300

Bol Garang Akon, $250 equivalent to one cattle

Elizabeth Sama Mayeen, $150

I owe a big thank you to these people due to their outstanding contribution to my marriage. It meant a lot to me. People like Mr Malith Makuch continued to support me not only here but back home also when I returned for a second time.

Chapter 22

The Wedding Day

The wedding was organised back home, ahead of my arrival in South Sudan, because financially I was struggling to afford a ticket to the South Sudan to attend the wedding on the scheduled day. Therefore, I wasn't sure whether I would be there on time or not. Thanks, God everything was wonderful even though I wasn't there.

My half-brothers, under Mr Georgy Agany's administration, could pay the rest of the cows to my in-laws. Despite the challenges that people faced in attending the wedding, such as a lack of transport, the few who attended enjoyed it immensely. I was in contact with Mr Athain and my wife each day until of the end of the three days of the wedding. Overall, it was a wonderful wedding, and I was the only one who was missing for that significant event. But, after the wedding, Abuk's family took her to where her new family lived, to my half-brother's house in Maphiir Aweer, Aweil. I found her there when I arrived in April 2013 after I organised myself financially.

One week after the wedding, I left from the Perth International Airport to the Kenyan capital city of Nairobi. I give special thanks to Mr Garang Tong Khon for helping me to get to the airport at four o'clock in the morning because, at that time of day, all friends and relatives refused to help, except him. Well done Mr Garang Tong, for your braveness. There aren't many people like him nowadays!

As I said, I left Perth on 25 March 2013 and reached the Kenyan capital as my first destination on the same day. I was met by Bol Aher. It was midnight, so I couldn't view the city properly, but inside Kenyatta International Airport, the view was pretty. At the airport, they spoke both English and their local language called Swahili. Unfortunately, I don't know that east African language, but I spoke with them in English. I found them to be very good at English; they speak it proficiently. As soon I finished my exit process, I found Mr Bol waiting. He greeted me warmly and welcomed me to Kenya for the first time. I thanked him for waiting for me. From there we took a taxi and went to Garang Aher's mother's house. I received a wonderful welcome from Diing Aher Garan's half-brother, Abuk Aher Garang's half-sister and more importantly, his mother, Ayeendit.

We spent all night talking to each other. They kept asking about their son, Mr Garang Aher, and the general situation in Australia. In return, I asked them how things were in Kenya, in terms of security and other factors because I was planning to bring my mother and my wife here for Abuk's process to be completed. 'Everything here is good, and I hope your family likes it. Don't worry, they won't be alone. We are all going to be there for any kind of help they might need,' Garang's mother told me.

During those two days, I could see how well established and beautiful Kenya's cities were. I became more motivated and confident to bring my family to Kenya. I stayed there for only two days and left Kenyatta Airport again to Juba International Airport on 27 March 2013 and reached Juba in only one and a half hours. There, I was well-received by my brother, Agany Atak.

Agany and I went to Kout Agany's house, where I had stayed before. Again, I was there for two days, and I left for Aweil town

Chapter 22   The Wedding Day

by plane because I planned this time by securing a ticket before I even left Australia. At Aweil domestic airport, I was expecting my wife Abuk to receive me, but unfortunately, she could not be there because she was taking care of Athain's sick wife. I understood the situation, and her apology was well-received. I thanked God I was greeted by my half-brother, Athain Atak; that alone meant so much to me. When I was about to enter the house, Abuk saw me from a long distance and ran towards me. We embraced with love and gave each other a huge hug.

That moment, everyone on the street stopped what they were doing and watched us. It was an amazing moment my wife and I won't forget. The only thing we didn't do was kiss each other because it is prohibited in our culture for a couple to do that in public. It sends a bad signal to the young ones. Apart from that, it was the most beautiful reunion that two lovers could dream of.

In the meantime, I received a warm welcome and greeting from Athain's family and neighbours. I thanked them so much for the outstanding welcome. In the morning, I spoke with my mother in Arieth, in Aweil's Northern part. At the same time, I went to visit Abuk's family, especially her mother who was not far away from where I was at that time. After two days, Abuk and I went to Arieth where my mother was living – my last destination.

We arrived there at 4.00 pm. There was no great reception at the bus station, like the previous year. From the bus station, we walked to the village, due to the lack of transport in that area. At home, we were welcomed by the family. My mother was so glad to see me again within one year. That night, we had a small family discussion. I told them I planned to take Abuk to Nairobi this time, where she will complete the documents to go to Australia. The whole family agreed it was a good idea because I could not live alone in diaspora anymore while I have a wife. 'We hope that God helps her so that the process can be done in a short period,' the family said. The second thing we talked about was who will join Abuk in Kenya because she cannot be there alone. I told them I wanted my mother to come with us and, after Abuk leaves, she would come back. But I needed two kids to help them both there in the meantime. I would put these kids into school for full-time study. Then George told me, 'You take Athain's daughter, Amiira, and my boy, Agany.'

'I accepted it. It's a done deal,' I told him. 'But here is the thing, Abuk and I will leave Arieth in two days, to Aweil, and go straight to Nairobi to submit her application form. The rest will come later, including my mother, because I don't want to waste any time.'

'You move on, man. God will help,' they said.

That is exactly what happened. In two days, we left Arieth, after I asked Athain to book tickets for us to Juba, and we arrived at Athain's house in the evening. After two days, we left by plane for Kout's house in Juba.

We stayed in Juba for four days. Then we booked two tickets to Kenya's capital. At 5.00 pm Kenya time, we arrived in the Kenya Airport. Again, I was received by Bol Aher, the man who had done so much for me.

We wasted no time. We went to the Australian Embassy and submitted Abuk's application form. After one week, they sent me the file number of the application. After some days, my wife and I rented our own property in the same area where Garang Aher's family was located. At that time, I started to do my best to make sure I brought in my mother before I left, as it would be very difficult for Abuk if I left her alone. While I was doing that, I realised I didn't have enough money. I called many friends and relatives to give me a hand and, thank God, a lot of friends and relatives responded to my call positively and gave me the help I was looking for. I thanked them so much for their generosity. One week before I left Kenya, my mother,

Chapter 22 The Wedding Day

Agany and Amiira arrived by bus in the capital city of Kenya. It was excellent to have Mother along with Abuk. My mother didn't like Kenya when she arrived there, and she kept asking me a lot of questions.

Two days before I left Nairobi, Abuk was confirmed pregnant, after I took her to the hospital when she felt sick. I was so delighted to hear such wonderful news! I couldn't believe I was going to be a father in the coming months! My mother was also crying with joy and happiness after she heard the news. Kenya, in general, was an awesome country, but they kept scaring people by telling us that, at night, thieves can attack you while you are sleeping and take everything you have. My wife was scared about this, even though I did my best to calm her down. Sometimes, I could see the threat of thieving was real, but there was nothing anyone like me could do about it. Other than that, Kenya is a very nice country and its views are fascinating – no question about it!

On 17 March 2013, I left the republic of Kenya, hoping the Department of Immigration would speed up my wife's process so that she could arrive in Australia as soon as possible, and give my mother a chance to go back to South Sudan to take care of the rest of my brothers and sisters. The next day I arrived in Perth. This time, there was no reception from my friends and colleagues because they were too busy.

My arrival to Perth that time wasn't different from the previous one. I still struggled to find a job. I went to so many agents, and they told me to be patient. This was the most difficult time in my life. No job and no money, while at the same time I had to pay two rents. The first rent was the Kenya property where my family lived. The second one was the Balga accommodation, plus food for myself and those who were living in Nairobi. The one source of income I had at that time was Centrelink money, which was not enough. I took loans from different sources, such as friends, Cash Converters and other private institutions.

I was always worried and anxious about everything. I tried to read Roy T. Bennet's statement every day, which says, 'It's important what thoughts you are feeding into your mind because your thoughts create your belief and experiences. You have positive thoughts, and you have negative ones too. Nurture your mind with positive thoughts: kindness, empathy, compassion, peace, love, joy, humility, generosity, etc. The more you feed your mind with positive thoughts, the more you can attract great things into your life.' It was a very good message, but I couldn't listen to it.

My mind was always busy. How do I pay my rent tomorrow? How do I pay the Nairobi rent? My mind was completely restless during that period and to make matters worse, Abuk was very sick, due to her pregnancy. Her body didn't respond positively, and every time she saw a doctor, whether for her routine check-up or a different issue, she spent too much money. Doctors were taking too much from her because they knew her husband was in diaspora, therefore, no matter what, she would pay. It was disgusting and unacceptable behaviour from them because not everyone in diaspora has money.

When Abuk was four months and 15 days pregnant, she miscarried her first daughter, in unprecedented circumstances. I was trying to understand exactly what happened from the doctors, but they didn't give me much information. She was hospitalised in the Nairobi women's hospital for three days, where one day was more than $100 US. It was a horrible situation I found myself in, but thanks to Brother Diing Aher and Abuk Aher for their great assistance because without them I'm sure things would have been more difficult than they were. They spent all their time in the hospital and updated me on everything that was happening to Abuk. My phone was very busy during those three days. Again, I could take another loan from Cash Converters to pay the money. I talked to Abuk about leaving all this to God, and He would help. Unfortunately, she

Chapter 22 The Wedding Day

didn't listen and kept crying all day. I started to be worried about her health, and I prayed every day for her emigration papers to be processed quickly. It was overwhelmingly stressful and fearful to the extent that I couldn't sleep at night because my mind was too anxious.

In July 2013, I secured a casual job at Vesco Food. It was a big help, even though I was only working three days. In August 2013, Abuk was sent to the medical centre. She completed the medical process twice, and was asked to repeat some of it. From that moment, she changed completely because she started to have hope. She started to eat and take care of herself again. I felt that her change was because of the conversations we had during that period.

On 20 November 2013, at 4.30 pm, I got an important email from the Department of Border Protection that said: 'Congratulations sir, your partner, Abuk Kuach, has been granted a visa to come to Australia. Her tickets are your full responsibility, and you have six months to obtain them before the expiry of the visa.' Oh my God, I couldn't believe it! I was so delighted, I called Abuk and told her the great news. She was silent for a minute. I said, 'Abuk are you there?'

But there was no answer at all until she said, 'I'm here,' and she started to talk. I could feel she was crying. From there, I told her I had to leave her and would she please inform my mother with this great news because I was at work at that moment. However, that day I left work early and tried to think wisely about how I would get Abuk's ticket.

At night, I called Abuk again, and I told her to give the phone to my mother. When she did, my mother told me that she was so happy and urged me to do something very fast to secure Abuk's ticket. 'When your wife heard that her visa had been issued, she was crying, dancing and confused. She didn't know what to do because she has suffered a lot. I think right now is a good moment for her to see good things,' mother said.

'No worries,' I said. 'Now, I don't have money for her ticket, but I will do my best to secure it, in God's will,' I told her.

'Go ahead, son, God will be there to help you,' mother said.

After that, I ended the conversation because I had a lot do that night. In two days, I called Mr John Atem and asked him to help me with a ticket, and I would pay him back after Abuk's arrival. He agreed and sent $3000 to my account instantly. I gave him a big thank you and wasted no time. I booked a ticket for Abuk to arrive in Perth on 13 December 2013. When Abuk and my mother heard that magnificent news, their happiness increased. I informed the entire family in South Sudan and here in Australia about the arrival of Abuk. But, she was doing too much shopping in Nairobi city, and it cost me a lot of money without her realising it.

Before her arrival, I arranged many things. I spoke with Mr Akol Akol and his wife, Akech Mou, so that my wife could be in their accommodation for some weeks, before I took her to where I lived. I did so because I'm always very busy and it would be very difficult to leave her alone. Akol Akol's consent made things very easy for me. I talked to everyone I knew in WA to help me financially, while I was preparing for welcoming Abuk to Akol Akol's house. Thank God, they agreed and responded positively. I told my mother to be ready because after the departure of Abuk, they would leave Kenya's capital immediately because she always claimed she missed South Sudan so much. Both Amiir and Agany, who were with my mother and wife, didn't have to enrol in their respective schools again because they were leaving.

On 12 December 2013, Abuk left the capital by Emirate Airlines. Everyone was worried about her because she had never travelled that distance alone. I was worried too. I kept praying to God to bring her here safely. I spoke to her multiple times before she left and told her exactly what to do if she got lost or confused. The good thing was that her Arabic language

Chapter 22 The Wedding Day

was very good and would help her at Dobie International Airport, her only transit before she arrived here. According to her ticket, she would arrive at Perth International Airport, at 4.30 pm local time, the following day. That night I struggled to get some sleep because I was so happy for her coming. At the same time, I was worried too by all the 'ifs.' For example, what would I do if she could not make it to Australia? Who would I contact to help me out? What would I say to her Mother? And so on and so on...

In the morning, I washed my old car and made it look wonderful, ready to go and pick up my beautiful wife at the airport that afternoon. I had been contacted by a lot of people who were wondering about her arrival. During that time, I was very busy with WA Aweil ladies because they kept sending me shopping to prepare all necessities for the gathering. I thanked them so much, although they gave me a hard time by keeping me busy they did an incredible job. They contributed a lot financially and prepared all kind of foods and drinks for the visitors. I was so lucky and blessed to get that wonderful help from them. They made me so proud that night!

At three o'clock, Thiik Deng Riiny and I went to the Perth Airport. We were joined by his wife, plus two other women. These ladies helped me so much. They reminded me to take flowers with me to give to Abuk as soon she arrived. Thank God, we bought some on our way to the airport. Inside the airport, I was worried. Everyone else was sitting in his or her chair, except me. I couldn't do that because I was eager to see Abuk as soon as possible. Every time I saw people coming out, I expected to see Abuk, and when I didn't see her, I felt disappointed. While I was doing that, I kept looking at flight numbers to see when it would arrive. In the end, we were told the plane would arrive late, which increased my anxiety. The only option was to wait! At 5.30 pm we were informed the plane was touching down. Therefore, they will be out soon.

Then I started to take some breaths, but was soon worried again because I was scared I might find out at the end that Abuk had missed this plane, which would be very difficult for me to deal with.

However, a huge number of people started to come out of that plane, but Abuk still was not coming out. 'What is going on?' I asked my friend. 'Calm down, Deng, everything will be good. Let us keep waiting,' Thiik said.

'Waiting? I cannot wait anymore!' I said.

'No way, we must wait, man,' Thiik replied. I hated the word 'wait.' As I kept my focus on those coming out and looked at them one by one, I finally saw Abuk among them. I ran toward her, and she did the same when she saw me. We gave each other an unforgettable hug but no kissing, as I mentioned before, since we don't usually do this in public as part of our culture and tradition. I gave her the flowers. Thiik and the rest took that opportunity to take a photo of us. It was fantastic, and all my negative thoughts went away. I was relieved when I found Abuk safe and awesome. From there, we came out from the airport to where our cars were and drove home.

At home, she was welcomed by the Aweil community members. She then took some rest. I then asked her to come out and introduce herself to the people of Western Australia, in one of the best environments ever. That night, I called her relatives in Juba, South Sudan to inform them of her safe arrival. I used this opportunity to inform those who were in Kenya as well, my Mother and Garang Aher's mother. The following day, I took her to Centrelink and other important institutions in WA. In the mean-time I took her to visit some Aweil houses.

On 15 December 2013, I received a phone call in the early morning from one of our elders, Adup Aguer Ngor, telling me that there was a war going on right now in Juba. 'What? Who is fighting who?' I asked.

Chapter 22 The Wedding Day

'I don't know. They are waiting for clarification from the president's office,' he replied. After that, I didn't sleep anymore. I called my brother Agany to find out exactly what was going on, but he said he had no idea. 'Look, Deng, there is too much bombardment everywhere in Juba, and we don't know who is actually fighting who. Some people keep saying it is a coup,' Agany said.

'Please don't go out because it is too dangerous and take care,' I told him.

'No problem,' he replied.

In the afternoon, while we were watching South Sudanese TV, President Kiir appear on TV he said that there was a coup attempt, orchestrated by Mr Reik Machar and his colleagues, without giving more details on how this happened. This left so many unanswered questions hanging in the air. From that moment, we started to disagree with what the president had said. Some agreed with the president and called it a 'coup attempt' but the rest, myself included chose not to buy into the 'coup attempt' the president had announced, because it lacked credibility and evidence. Following that, the violence spread into the flashpoint town of Bor, the capital of eastern Jonglei state, and in Torit, the capital of Eastern Equatoria. A lot of lives were lost, and people found themselves in a chaotic environment.

A few days later, the ex-Vice President, Reik Machar, appeared on social media and denied the president's allegations and accusations. That was fair enough, but he went on and made a historic mistake when he chose to join his tribe who was fighting the Juba government for the revenge of their families and friends they claimed had been killed in Juba. In my opinion, Mr Machar should have distanced himself from this, after president Kiir's coup attempt had been rejected internationally, and then look for another safe country for him and his family.

At least he would have silenced the doubters and those who used to claim that Machar did it in 1991 and again in 2013.

He would win the peoples' heart, especially those who love peace, not war. However, the majority knew, including those in government, of the lack of credibility of the coup attempt announced by his Excellency, the president of the Republic. But Reik helped him out when he chose a wrong path to resolve the conflict. As Mr Machar started to engage himself fully in the war with his tribe, and President Kiir on another side with his tribe as well, the situation turned horrific and was devastating for all South Sudanese, particularly those who were living in the war zone. In the diaspora, South Sudanese people were debating in every corner they met, whether what happened on 15.12.2015 was a coup.

As my wife enjoyed her new country, I was worried about how I would repay my loans. I owed a lot of people, plus the Commonwealth Bank. The situation in South Sudan was worrying as well because the nation was war-torn, and it concerned everyone, especially those who had loved ones there. I have relatives and friends there, and as the conflict changed from political disputes to tribal war between my own tribe (Dinka) and Reik Machar's tribe (Nuer), many innocent and vulnerable people suffered.

Between the BBC reports and YouTube, we could see how South Sudanese people killed each other brutally, without mercy or brotherhood.

As I saw people turn the conflict between President Kiir and Dr Reik Machar into a tribal war, I wrote this strong message, on my Facebook account, to the Southerners around the world.

Chapter 23

Lessons for the Future

Our diversity is our strength and decency! My fellow South Sudanese people, I'm sure our existence, with a lot of differences among our cultures and traditions, in this lovely land called South Sudan is not a coincidence or a curse, but it is a blessing, and it is God's wisdom that we should be there with all these distinctions! God has known us before he put us there. According to my understanding, whatever God does, he always does it with grace and a great purpose because God's ways are not human's ways. So, we should accept ourselves and live with love, respect and harmony.

My dear 64 tribes in South Sudan, I'm sure we have been talking about what is separating us and bringing hatred among us for so long now. I suggest it is the right time to stop exercising those 'unacceptable behaviours.' I'm sure this difficult time will go, and we will end up victorious in God's name. Those who are practising oppression and bigotry will go. It is just a matter of time, as Mahatma Gandhi once said: 'When I despair, I remember that all through history the way of truth and love has always won. There have been tyrants and murderers, and for a time, they can seem invincible, but in the end, they always fall. Think of it always."

So, my brothers and sisters in my beloved country, do not lose hope. Start right now to promote what can bring us together instead of what can demote our cohesive unity. We all have a beautiful culture that we should be proud of and focus on it; one that you cannot find anywhere else in the world. For example, we all respect our elders and mothers, we also have the most staggering dance groups in east Africa, if not the whole Africa and we are also proud of our ancestors.

However, I know we lack genuine leaders now, since we lost the late Dr John Garang. The current leaders are not doing enough to bring us together. Instead, they're focusing on their own tribes and leaving the rest to suffer and be humiliated.

Let us forget about what the current leaders are doing now because they stack already and they have taken us now to be more like 'Somalia' and that is a fact whether they accept it or not. They are just there to get their salaries, but they don't have strong strategies or a good plan to take us out of this horrifying situation.

Lastly, let us forgive each other and give ourselves a chance for real peace and reconciliation, for the sake of this country. For us to move forward, as Max De Pree said: 'We need to give each other the space to grow, to be ourselves, to exercise our diversity. We need to give each other space so that we may both give and receive such beautiful things as ideas, openness, dignity, joy, healing and inclusion.

Unfortunately, no one listened because everyone wanted to defend his opponent military. On 25 December 2013, I celebrated the first Christmas ever with my wife, at Saint Bakhita Church. I prayed a lot that Christmas and asked God to bless my new family. I hoped my wife did the same thing also. She was warmly welcomed by Saint Bakhita believers, without exception. They all congratulated me on my marriage and for being able to choose such a wonderful, social and beautiful girl like Abuk Kuach

Chapter 23 Lessons for the Future

Many people kept telling me 'Deng, you are a very smart boy, and you know how to select a good one, man!' Some believers managed to visit me at Akol Akol's house, at Girraween, to continue congratulating me and gave us so much advice, as a new couple who are new on their journey.

However, I only spent two months in Akol Akol's accommodation before I moved to my own house in Balga. There, I kept watching and listening carefully to South Sudan news because the situation was getting worse day after day. Every day before I went to bed, I had to make sure I called all the relatives in South Sudan, especially those who were in Juba. In the meantime, I was receiving enormous pressure from the people who wanted their money back because I did promise them that as soon my wife arrived their monies would be returned. I thought I would get another job with good pay to help clear all the loans but, regrettably, nothing changed except the arrival of my wife. No new job and my current job was getting low. That made things very difficult for me. But, thank God for giving me Abuk as my wife because she is the nicest, most humble woman anyone in my situation could hope to have. She didn't care so much about money, whether we had it or not; what she wanted was only for me to be at home. She was praying so much, every day, for God to help us and she was very happy and satisfied with the small money I provided to her. I continued to struggle financially, I kept looking for a good job in the meantime.

On 9 February 2014, I received a phone call from Garang Aher's mother telling me that my mother had been hospitalised because she was very sick. It was midnight, and I didn't have enough credit on my phone, so I told her I would call tomorrow. That night, I informed Abuk about what was going on. In the morning, I called Garang Aher's mother, and I asked her to give the phone to my mother. As I spoke to her, she told me that she used to be very sick, but thank God, was very good now. 'That's good news!' I said, 'but what happened?' I asked.

'I don't know, but I had a severe headache, pain everywhere and before I knew it, I found myself in the hospital. I was told that I was unconscious,' my mother said.

'Okay, no problem. You get some rest,' I said.

When I talked to the hospital, they told me they needed $500 US for her to be discharged from the hospital. That was too much for me because at that time it was equal to $750 AU.

I was furious and asked them, 'Why?'

'We don't know sir, but you have to pay or we won't release your mother,' they said. I ended the conversation with them, and my mind stopped working because I didn't know where I would get the money.

From that time, I learnt a very important lesson: When good things keep happening in your life, they won't stop easily, and when bad things take space in your life, they also won't stop easily.

This is exactly what happened to me because I needed money to pay those who wanted money from me. At the same time, I was still facing some difficulties and challenges that could also end up needing money and increasing my burden. Some days later, I was able to get another loan from my friends and sent the money to my mother. From there, they discharged her with some medication to use. When I talked to my mother, she told me she is now fine. 'I'm sorry I gave you a hard time, even though I knew what difficulty you are in,' mother said.

'Don't worry,' I told her. 'If I don't suffer and do my best for you, then who else would?'

Chapter 23 Lessons for the Future

'My son, they did this to you because they knew you are living in Australia. Therefore, they were confident you would pay,' she said.

'No problem, but you are not going to stay there any longer because, in two weeks' time, you have to go back to South Sudan.' This is exactly what happened. I borrowed more money from Cash Converters and sent it to her. They booked their flight, and on 13 March 2014, they left Kenya's capital and arrived in Juba the same day. They stayed there for only two weeks before they went to Aweil city and from there they went to my village, Arieth.

Politically, I was frustrated with both President Kiir and his former vice president, Dr Reik Machar, for not being able to end the unnecessary war that killed Southerners day in and day out. In addition, the SPLM party, which included President Kiir and Dr Reik Machar, did a good job by helping south Sudanese people to have a chance at establishing their own country. But, they messed up too much in the process, which led me to write this on my Facebook account to the southerners on 15 September 2014:

SPLM/SPLA is an emancipator and deadly!

Dear South Sudanese people, history will acknowledge how SPLM/SPLA struggled and fought with a combination of 'talent and determination.' I mean, they gave it all to let us have what the world supported in 2011, the new country called 'South Sudan.' Without doubt, the world has received us with 'open arms, a lot of enthusiasm and hope'. All South Sudanese, wherever they are, were so 'proud and optimistic' at that time. That was an incredible and huge achievement by SPLM/SPLA, which will not be forgotten for many years to come!

However, history will make enormous mistakes if it fails to mention that it is the same SPLM/SPLA that made all these sacrifices and conquered the impossible Khartoum regime, which brought South Sudan, as a country, to its knees three years later, after they had liberated their people from the most oppressive regime the world had ever seen, they decided to fight each other and brought a senseless war to the South Sudanese people, particularly the vulnerable citizens who cannot even afford their daily bread.

The SPLM/SPLA has failed completely to handle their differences in their own room (party).It was shameful, disgusting and shocking when they took the wrong path and divided themselves according to their tribes and ethnicities and forgot what they fought for. What does SPLM/SPLA stand for? Who is the real enemy?

Moreover, because of that war, they put everyone in confusion. Some people thought it was Machar's unfinished business in 1991 to get SPLM/SPLA leadership, others thought it was revenge for what happened in 1991, and President Kiir said, in the last liberation council meeting before the war started, 'This is not going to be like 1991,' which meant he was right on that time.

In my opinion, it was a huge miscalculation by our brothers and sisters in the SPLM party to not be able to control the situation. It was also a conspiracy by those who have a special interest in our resources, but unfortunately, our leaders failed badly to recognise it because they were supposed to use proper and peaceful procedures to deal with it. Now, we're in a desperate and horrific situation, and our people are so exhausted and tired of this senseless war.

In my conclusion, the current leaders showed us that they are just self-interested and are not capable of leading us because they don't have the spirit of nationalism and patriotism. The real question is how long will the South Sudanese endure and forbear?

Chapter 23   Lessons for the Future

Nonetheless, 2015 was the best year ever for me. It was the year I could clear some loans after I successfully claimed my tax return and was given back $7000 as my refund. That was wonderful because after I cleared the loans, I felt relief from the pressure I had been under, even though these amounts weren't enough to cover all the loans I received from others.

It was the same year that my wife felt sick, and when I took her to the GP Doctor, I was told: 'Congratulations, Sir, your wife is pregnant.' I was so delighted and joyful with that news because in the coming months, I would be a father.

It sounded very nice to me, and I thanked Almighty God for that wonderful gift. It meant a lot to me. On the other hand, my wife was crying to express her happiness and at the same time, she was worried that she might again miscarry.

But I encouraged her to be strong because things are different here, 'First, I'm here. Plus, the medical facilities in Australia are far more advanced than those in Africa. Therefore, none of the things that happened to you when you were in Nairobi will happen easily here, in Australia. Trust me and trust what I say, and you and your baby will be okay.' As she listened to me, she started to feel confident. She was also attending regular monthly check-ups.

In the same year, I was elected Secretary for the Electoral Committee of the Aweil Community Association, in WA, with Tamim Abdulrahman as the Chairperson. We had a successful election, and we announced Mr James Amoi as the new Aweil community leader in WA, to follow on from Mr Deng Deng Mou.

In my normal life, I realised that the South Sudanese had changed completely from the way they used to be, which is stating the truth, no matter what. Therefore, as usual, I used my Facebook account to give them a wake-up call with this title:

Why is it hard for Southerners to speak the truth nowadays?

My fellow Southerners, according to my knowledge and understanding, speaking 'truth' is one of the basic and fundamental norms we exercise daily, in our cultural activities as Southerners. In other words, speaking the truth is part of us.

To go further, I can say with strong conviction that we learned how to speak the truth through our fathers and grandfathers because they were in full control of their affairs, by confronting each other through telling themselves the 'truth'.

My brothers and sisters in the republic of South Sudan, whether you agree on this or not, I can say that we have failed completely to speak the 'truth' to our leaders, our fellow citizens and ourselves since the conflict erupted in our country three years ago. And, by doing just that, we have contributed by shape or form to the destruction and ruining of our own beloved country.

However, the truth itself is undeniable, whether you say it or not, it will reveal itself in time, as Buddha illustrated 'three things cannot be long hidden: the Sun, the Moon and the Truth.'

I'm saying all this because some people decided, during this conflict, to be pro-President Kiir, not because his is right and elected president, but because they wanted to please Kiir for future references. Some people are scared to death to speak the truth, especially those who are in Juba, because those who did, have lost their lives already. Some people consider President Kiir to be from their tribe, therefore, they must show loyalty to Kiir, no matter what. Some people refused to tell the truth because they didn't want to be labelled as 'rebel and opposition' if they are not from the President's tribe, or seen as 'traitors and betrayers' if they are from Kiir's tribe.

Moreover, I'm sure the same things are happening to those who are supporting Reik Machar. They're just doing it because they consider themselves to be from Machar's tribe, or scared to be labelled as 'betrayers and traitors'. This is unacceptable, my fellow citizens. If we continue doing that, it will be hard for

Chapter 23　Lessons for the Future

everyone to separate between our tribes and politics, political parties and our ethnicities.

In conclusion, I'm sure some people are not speaking the 'truth' because they don't know it. Our leaders are not telling the truth. Sometimes, even the media around us are not giving accurate information, and that makes it difficult for everyone to pick up the truth straight away. As Eris Murdoch put it, 'We live in a fantasy world, a world of illusion. The great task in life is to find reality.

My lovely wife, Abuk Kuach, delivered my little son, Agany Deng Atak on 5 November 2015. It was an unforgettable day. I remember that day as being the most difficult moment for me, especially when the doctors decided to deliver the baby by operation to get the child out as soon as possible because the baby was at risk, according to them. They gave me a document to sign for the operation to go ahead. I was so scared because I was worried about the well-being and health of Abuk, as well as the baby, and what could happen to her if she went through the operation. But thank God Elizabeth Sama Moyeen was there with her husband and they gave me enormous support. They told me to sign the paper and leave the rest to God. So, without any more hesitation, I signed it and they operated successfully in less than 45 minutes and baby, Agany, came out in good health, and his mother was doing tremendously well also.

I then called the relatives and friends to inform them about the great news of me being a dad for the first time in my life. My relatives at home, in South Sudan, told me to call the baby Agany, which is my last name and is my grandfather's name too. The baby and his mother stayed there, in Osborn Park Hospital, for some days before they were discharged. During that period, Elizabeth Sama did a great job by visiting them every day with fruits and the sort of foods that are needed for the mother in that stage. Not only that, but she was there every day at home, after we left the hospital, teaching Abuk how to give a shower to a new baby like Agany. To be frank, I think I will be owing Elizabeth and her family a big thank you all my life for the sacrifices, services, assistance and advice they gave me and my little family. They made me feel like I was at home with my brothers, sisters and mother.

Again, I kept writing on my Facebook, hoping that I could advise people to do the right thing. This is what I wrote:

What is going on in our beloved South Sudan?

Since the conflict erupted in the Republic of South Sudan three years ago, we have seen, heard and witnessed the despicable acts and misbehaviour of some people.

Our government and its supporters have shifted 90 degrees in their moral obligations, and have started to categorise South Sudanese as Pro-Kiir or Pro-Machar and nothing else in between. So, you either support President Kiir and consider yourself a 'nationalist' or you end up as a rebel, traitor, betrayer, etc.

Saying that, you can see how poisoned, sophisticated and chaotic our social status and political environment has become. Moreover, nowadays if you don't support President Kiir 's government and his policy, knowing they're doing nothing regarding moving the country forward, then you're not just in opposition, but you're a rebel, whether you like it or not, according to Kiir's strong supporters.

However, if you criticise both camps (Kiir-Machar), you will be labelled as a hypocrite and opportunist. If you stood with the South Sudan as a nation and distanced yourself from both camps, then you made the most enormous mistake in your entire life because, according to Kiir's supporters, they think you should have respect and loyalty to President Kiir first, before the nation.

The situation is deteriorating day after day. Imagine, even those who are just peacefully protesting, demanding their rights, or questioning why their salaries have been away for so long, can be labelled as SPLM-IO supporters and could face charges, such as treason, etc., which is absolutely disgusting!

Lastly, I'm sure our people learned this oppression from the Khartoum system because those who were in Sudan knew it very well. If you protest or complain, and you're from South Sudan, you will be labelled as a rebel and pro-Garang, whether you accept it or not. It seems our government is following the same footsteps by doing their utmost to replicate what they saw previously.

In my perspective, that kind of act from the government and its subordinates is part of denying people's rights, by frightening them and showing intimidation tactics.

Leadership is not something easy, as some think, it requires wisdom and open-mindedness. William Arthur Wood once said: 'Leadership is based on inspiration, not domination; on cooperation, not intimidation.'

Does South Sudan benefit from its intellectual and well-educated people? If not, why not?

My fellow South Sudanese people, Mr Kofi Annan, Former United Nations General-Secretary, once said: 'Knowledge is power. Information is liberating, education is the premise of progress, in every society, in every family.' Unfortunately, those wise and beautiful words from his Excellency are not reflecting in our situation today, because what we are seeing is completely opposite from what he admired and predicted to happen everywhere around the world, and our nation is included.

Ladies and gentlemen, let us be frank. Apart from Dr Reik Machar's case, if we look deep down, we'll see those who are well-educated are struggling to find their spaces in South

Sudan's political arena, and a majority of them are outside the country without mentioning their names. Those who decide to remain in the country are working with the government as numbers and representatives, and they are working with caution to make sure their voices cannot be heard otherwise, as they can be excluded immediately without mercy. The rest are helpless, and they are watching with stillness.

Some people used to say, 'We didn't liberate this country by education. Therefore, we don't care.' But, I entirely disagree with them because if the late Dr John Garang weren't such a well-educated person who illustrated the root cause of injustice we witnessed from the Khartoum regime and demonstrated that, not only to us but to the entire world, we wouldn't convince ourselves that we had a genuine issue to fight for.

With that said, many people are alarmed with the situation, and they're raising many questions:

1. Has South Sudan been hijacked by an uneducated group? Or was education itself cursed a long time ago, and those who are highly educated cannot deliver, no matter what?

2. How on earth do we expect our country to be developed, when we want to get rid of those with such knowledge?

Lastly, I have a firm conviction that we all need everyone on this journey to devolvement and prosperity, educated and uneducated, just as we need a good arrangement to make sure the right man/woman is in the right position.

For everyone's information, there's no way we can disregard the significance of education and what it can do to transform our nation into a better and more competitive South Sudan. Education helps one form fortified new ideas and build upon them to give back to the community and the nation.

How can we avoid school if it teaches men/women to think about different perspectives, look at things with divergent

Chapter 23 Lessons for the Future

views and reach conclusions that will first help him and then those around him?

In other words, my fellow South Sudanese, a nation filled with educated men and women is a nation full of the potential to impact progress around itself.

In 2016, I decided to go back to finish my studies, so I applied to Curtin University to do International Relations because I found myself lacking a strong passion for continuing with Accounting, even though I was confident that I could do it successfully. While I was waiting for my admission from Curtin's administration, I kept up with my activities on **Facebook**, and this is what I wrote:

Are we struggling to differentiate political and non-political organisation activities from personal relationship and social gathering activities?

My dear South Sudanese people around the globe, nowadays a lot of South Sudanese people are struggling to get this equation I mentioned above right.

It astonishes me and raises so many questions in my head, such as:

1. Are we new to this sophisticated environment of how to build both community activities and personal relationships so that they go together smoothly, without harming ourselves and others, especially the vulnerable ones?

2. Are we really fit to handle this? Or maybe it is too big for us, and whatever we're going to do regarding this issue will be short to make it happen?

3. Why can't those who call themselves intellectuals organise a workshop to explain to people how this operates?

Personally, I can say with confidence that this issue is problematic. Therefore, we must find a real and quick solution to protect our next generation from this disease.

However, according to my experience, some people don't know how to separate between community stuff and its belongings and their personal relationships with friends, colleagues, relatives, families and other community members. If someone has a personal problem with one of the community members, then he cannot wait for a community meeting or gathering to complicate things during the decision-making process.

To make matters worse, as soon as other people disagree with you on something, during a community meeting, then they take it personally, whether you like it or not. From then on, it will be tough for them to talk to you anymore, and they may go further and stop greeting you, which is absolutely disgusting! But this is a very unfortunate situation someone can find himself in. Moreover, some intellectuals are well informed regarding this issue, and they preach it to others, but they know, deep down, they cannot deliver.

When they have a problem, people expect a lot from them or to act more responsibly and set a good example for the rest to follow. Haplessly, they mess up and fail badly every time they have been tested. Those who can handle this heavy burden in our communities today are numbered. Therefore, I offer my sincere salute before them.

Some weeks later, I wrote another article on my Facebook account when I realised that my community's morale and our decency culture had been tested and challenged, particularly those who were exhibiting unacceptable behaviour online and were sending a bad image of Aweilians.

Chapter 23   Lessons for the Future

In that regard, I wrote this:

Denigrating and disrespecting ourselves won't take us anywhere.

My fellow Aweilians in Australia, the land of opportunity, and particularly our women/mothers in the Eastern States, we keep listening to your personal videos you share with us every day. Some are helpful, and some are woeful. With respect, I'm here to talk about the miserable ones. My mothers and my sisters, enough is enough! Please stop these bizarre insulting videos.

Please stop trying to finish yourself like that. If you don't need yourself, then remember that we, as the Aweil Community around the world, absolutely need you, your contributions, and your outstanding support in so many things that we are dealing with today and so do those who are waiting ahead of us. Please listen to me once, I beg you to stop taking yourself down, one by one, with unacceptable behaviour, it won't take you anywhere.

It is time you listen to us, right now, as your fathers, elders, husbands, families, sons, daughters, and most importantly your fellow Aweilians.

These live and recorded videos are horrible and disgusting, therefore, they must come to an end immediately. What are you going to get from this unacceptable and despicable act? What kind of legacy do you want to leave behind? What sort of legacy do you want to leave to your children and your grandchildren?

Be reminded that choosing to humiliate and abuse yourself and others with such brutality will send a wrong signal and bad picture, not only to your family but your relatives also. However, make no mistake about what you are doing today; it will be recorded as who you are, if you left this beautiful and wonderful world one day. If you don't change your behaviour and the way you treat your fellow women and others, then don't blame history tomorrow if all your goodwill and decency is disregarded.

My mothers and my sisters, please forgive me if I have been harsh and tough with you about this issue, but you left me with no other option. I cannot sit here and watch you damaging your reputations, your children's status and denigrate your grandchildren also. What you don't know is that these videos you produce, day in and day out on Facebook and other social media, will be there for many years to come.

Therefore, you must stop this, if not for your children and your family's fame, then stop it for the sake of all of us, as Aweil sons and daughters. This dirty job you're committing and engaging yourself in will be a huge challenge and bad record for the entire Aweil community around the world, which will take some years to overcome.

Lastly, I want to use this opportunity to appeal to the Chairman of Great Mading Aweil, Mr Simon Henry Angok, and the Eastern States Community leaders to do their utmost and collaborate among themselves to fix these small issues among our women. I'm confident you will make them live in love, harmony, respect and allegiance to themselves, first, as well as to the mighty Mading Aweil. I'm also appealing to our veteran and gallant elders, both men and women, to make sure they use proper techniques to consolidate peace and intimacy among our ladies.

My mothers, my sisters and my fellow Aweilians, I'm appealing to you all, for the last time, please stop this! Great Aweil executive body, Aweil elders in all States and Aweil Community States leaders, please, I beg you all - you must rectify this mess as soon as possible before it gets out of control. Please fix this, at any cost, before it is too late.

Chapter 23   Lessons for the Future

Finally, if you're friends with me on Facebook, please share this post with others, especially Aweil Community Leaders who are not friends, so that they can get my clear message. For our women who don't understand what I'm talking about, please find someone to help you out.

Politically, I also wrote this article on my **Facebook** *account:*

Sovereignty State!

My followers south Sudanese, we hear 'sovereignty state' quite often from our ministers in South Sudan, but they confuse me because I don't know what comes first, according to them - is it sovereignty or citizens?

They said, 'Action speaks louder than word.' So, our ministers, rather than just saying these words, should demonstrate them by taking care and protecting our people, come up with real solutions for the already suffering economy, promote unity and reconciliation among the citizens, rather than a divide and rule policy.

Both Kiir's supporters and Reik's supporters should put citizens first. Instead we are seeing Kiir's supporters busy with how to maintain and keep Kiir in power at any cost, and Reik's supporters are doing their utmost to install Machar in the presidency. They have all left our people to suffer and be displaced to the neighbouring countries, once again. This after we got our country and then claimed that we have 'sovereignty state'!

Lastly, rather than rejecting intervention forces and do nothing about the current conflict, we should come up with strong strategies to tell them that we have it under control, instead of pursuing Reik Machar in the equatorial forest. Come on guys, we can't run the country's affairs that way, and trust me, we're not going to prevent third party intervention if southerners are divided and fractionated.

Because I had been active on my Facebook account, criticising the Government of South Sudan and its subordinates, I was accused of being a Dr Reik Machar supporter, but I told them that I don't support him, nor do I support President Kiir. I'm just a concerned citizen who doesn't like the way the country is managed so far by its leaders.

In my personal life, I was given an offer by Curtin University, in 2017, to do an Art course. So, without hesitation, I accepted that course as a part-time student and full-time employee at Vesco Foods. It isn't easy, but this is what I'm doing now. I did my first week at Curtin, in a tremendous environment and with a lot of enthusiasm because I couldn't believe that I was finally able to attend university. The first lecture I attended was 'Legacies of Empire,' with over three hundred students. That moment was a special one for me because I was tearing-up, due to the joy and satisfaction of what I had accomplished so far. Without a doubt, I was the first person to enter university in my family, so it was a big dream, not only for me, but the entire Atak Ken family. I wish my dad could be alive today to see what I have achieved. Now, I have a big challenge to be able to finish what I started and obtain a degree in Art. Otherwise, it will be shameful.

Western Australia is a special and fantastic place for me. It is a place where I started to shine and make a name for myself. It is a place where I became confident and became somebody. During my time in Western Australia, I could carry out a successful program. For example, I have acted as Master of ceremony on several occasions in Australia, such as NSW and South Australia. Locally, I was the Aweil Master of ceremony of the first ever Aweil cultural day in Australia. I was master of ceremony for the wedding of brother Almeen, from Nubba Mountain, and his wife. I was master of ceremony of Makour Majock's wedding and his wife from Warrap State. I was also

Chapter 23 Lessons for the Future

MC for Aweil women's day, plus Adut Aher's concert in WA and many other activities.

On my facebook account, I put this strong message to my fellow South Sudanese people:

In order for us to move forward, we must stop these things:

Where were you when we fought more than two decades with the oppressive Khartoum regime?

Since its establishment, I have never betrayed SPLM/ SPLA, but some people did. I never ran away or left SPLM, not even a single day, but some did that also.

We didn't liberate this country through education. It doesn't matter how many qualifications you have; we won't employ you unless you join SPLM's long queue.

He deserved to be in parliament, even though he has no constituency, because his father did this and that.

Those who came back home from Khartoum are 'NCP and Arab,' therefore they are supposed to be treated as second-class citizens.

My tribe did a lot for this movement, and they are the reason we got our independence.

We, as SPLA, are the reason South Sudan got its independence because we brought a referendum to the Southerners.

We, as civilians of this beautiful land, are the reason we had our independence because we voted 99% for separation.

We are the best tribe in South Sudan because we are many and we are stronger; other tribes are 'nothing' because they didn't fight hard the way we did at struggle time.

My beloved South Sudanese people, the list above is responsible, directly or indirectly, for devastation and destruction of our young nation. If you are considering yourself great and you did a lot for this nation, then you don't have to reward yourself. If you do, then what will the people of South Sudan do?

However, if you pay attention to this list, you will realise that this list is mainly about 'I' did that or 'we' did this and that, therefore we need this and that. Nothing from people to say: 'You did this. Therefore, we recommend this for you.' Unbelievable guys! No country on earth can be run like this and stand long, no matter what.

The real nationalists and patriots are those who did a lot for their country, yet they are not willing to occupy any position as a reward. The real nationalists are those who are ready to resign, if that will make their nation better, and move forward.

For those who are about to lose hope, I put this message to them.

I have great hope for my beloved South Sudan!!!

After we witnessed and experienced long-suffering and painful moments from the 'most oppressive regime in African history,' we have been rewarded by having our own country, which we celebrated 6 years ago.

I'm sure many people will agree with me that we didn't get the country as a 'gift or donation,' as some friends quoted before me. In fact, we paid for it with our blood, lives, resources and livelihood.

My fellow South Sudanese people, since we earned our independence, our people, particularly the vulnerable, continue to suffer, day in and day out, because we opened a new chapter called 'the road toward a free, peaceful, democratic, devolved, stable and prosperous South Sudanese nation in east Africa' that we all hoped for.

Chapter 23 Lessons for the Future

My dear brothers and sisters in my beloved South Sudan, whether you agree with me or not, this new goal is harder and more difficult than the previous one, and it will cost us lives, more generations will miss education again, our dear ones will suffer and be humiliated terribly, for us to reach the second goal.

However, Mr Howard Zinn once said: 'There is no flag large enough to cover the shame of killing innocent people.' This is my strong message to those who are killing innocent people right now, to consider and think about it, because building South Sudan will require respect for each other, love and mercy for all. Everyone must obey the rules of law and the nation's constitution, including the president himself.

We all contributed, in shape or form, to the independence of the country. Therefore, we must salute and thank all our 64 tribes, for us to reach well, devolve and sustain a South Sudan of which we can all be proud.

Lastly, everyone, inside or outside the country, must contribute to the transformation of our beloved South Sudan into one of the best countries in the world. Yes, we <u>can</u> do that. Former US President, John F. Kennedy, once said: 'My fellow Americans, ask not what your country can do for you, ask what you can do for your country.'

My strong message to those who are supporting tribalism among the people is that there is no South Sudan without Nuer and Dinka, or Equatoria and Shul, or other tribes because each tribe has a unique role to play in nation-building, with deserved appreciation and acknowledgement.

Mr George Bernard Shaw once said: 'Patriotism is fundamental, a conviction that a particular country is the best in the world because you were born in it . . .'

On 10th May 2017, all South Sudanese people around the world, myself included, were shocked and surprised when South Sudan president sacked the powerful General Chief of Staff, Paul Malong. He was replaced with the Deputy Chief of General Staff for administration and finance, Lieutenant General James Ajongo Mawut.

General Paul is from my hometown Aweil state. His removal wasn't accepted well by his supporters especially my fellow Aweilians inside and outside the country. To make matters worse, Mr Paul Malong immediately left the capital Juba with a number of armed military officers after he got the news of his replacement on Tuesday night, while heading to his hometown Aweil. Unfortunately, he was stopped in Eastern Lakes state, Yirol.

However, that move by Mr Malong was misinterpreted by unconfirmed reports that Malong was heading to his hometown of Aweil to set up a military base. Aweil residents expressed fear there could be clashes between government forces and those allied with the general Paul Malong Awan. Many fled to rural areas for fear violence would break out. President Kiir did his best by appealing to South Sudanese around the world to remain calm, saying there will be no outbreak of violence after he fired Paul Malong. Some Aweilians who were abroad, prepared to write a condemnation letter to reject and denounce the president's decision of removing Mr Paul Malong. Some went behind and expressed their deep sorrow and disappointment with the president of the republic and the way he removed the general Paul.

With that being said, I used my Facebook account to express my view on this complicated issue and put it as a message to my fellow Aweilians as follows:

Chapter 23   Lessons for the Future

My message to Aweil Community leaders around the world

My fellow Aweilian around the world and particularly those who are in diaspora; I want to take this opportunity to warn our community leaders not to take unnecessary steps as a response to the recent relief of General Paul Malong Awan from his position as general chief of staff of SPLA by his Excellency the president of the Republic of South Sudan Kiir Mayardit.

I'm saying this because our community leaders in diaspora are planning to meet if not today then it will be tomorrow to discuss this divisive political issue which I think will be very hard for them to come up with a solution.

It is not in their mandate or their community Constitution, considering that our community organisations are non-political organisations, so there is no space for such topic unless they have nothing to do.

However, what they should know is that President has the constitutional power to relieve and elect without any pressure from anybody or community.

I'm sure when he elected Malong to this position he didn't consult the Aweil community citizens to have a voice on that, nor he appointed him (Malong) because he is from Aweil community.

We all know this man called president Kiir and his surprise decrees. We are also aware that both Kiir and Malong were friends for a long time. They mistreated so many Aweil sons horribly, and if their friendships exists no more, then let us distance ourselves from them otherwise, they will reconcile tomorrow, and the entire community will be the victim and pay the price.

Why is Malong so special? Put in mind that how many Aweil sons have been treated severely and fired by the president Kiir and we just said nothing about them, for example, we knew very well the recent story of Kuel Aguer Kuel and what both Kiir&Malong did to him.

Lastly, if there are any politicians out there who want to question the president, why he fired Paul Malong from his position? Then I reckon they have to call themselves Malong supporters instead of dragging the whole community with them for no reason.

Please exclude Aweil community from this because it is not a community issue but it is a political issue, and it is divisive. Therefore, there will be pro and against which is not going to be good for our cohesive unity.

Thank God my article was welcomed by so many Aweilians. A lot of people congratulated me on this. In the end, Aweil community abroad remains calm by choosing to do nothing on this matter.

Politically I keep giving pressure to our government back home hoping that they might change things. It is now four years on, and my country South Sudan is still unsettled.

President Kiir tried what he could do, but nothing has changed so far, in fact, things are turning from bad to worse.

The situation forces me to write this message on my home page as below:

What else is left for President Kiir Mayardit to do to make South Sudan develop and become a peaceful country?

My beloved South Sudanese people around the World, before and after the conflict that erupted in 2013, President Kiir did his best to remain in power by any costs. He also tried to make South Sudan a peaceful and stable country as part of his duties as a head of state.

Chapter 23   Lessons for the Future

Indeed he could maintain the power despite the loss of many lives and suffering of South Sudanese people across the country. Yes, he keeps the power despite many Southerners deciding not to live in South Sudan anymore because if they do, they will die by hunger and killer diseases. He kept the presidency by any cost despite so many misjudgements.

For example, when he pronounced what happened on date 15.12.2013 a coup attempt, without any of evidence to back it up. He went further and promised South Sudanese people that he would crush the opposition forces, but in the end, he couldn't. That was absolutely miscalculation from the president. Therefore, he should be made accountable for it.

In term of making South Sudan prosperous, peaceful and develop a stable economy, the president did his best, but unfortunately, none worked for him. He has made so many executive orders every day of firing ministers, generals, governors etc.

Appointing new faces in their places. This is exactly what is happening every day on South Sudan TV. It reaches beyond imagination because of nothing else on TV apart from a decree of relieving officials and appointing other people in their places.

At the end a lot of sorrow, the outcome is "zero." South Sudanese people and I are sick of that meaningless and madness decree on TV every night without real touchable changes. In fact, things are going from bad to worse. Nothing is working for his Excellency so far!

However, the logic that Mr president should know is that if things are not working well for him despite all changes he made, then he should be aware that he is incapable of appointing right people in the right positions. Therefore, he should consider himself part of failure also.

Lastly, in my own opinion, if all decrees the president made to relieve other people from their positions didn't improve the situation of South Sudan. Then why can't he do us a favour and decree himself out of presidency so that we can try someone else with new ideas, a new path and fresh blood. Who knows maybe this is what South Sudan needs in order, to prosper and thrive.

Moreover, when South Sudan's transitional Government were celebrating the sixth anniversary of the independence of the country from Khartoum. I realise that majority of the South Sudanese around the world and those overseas, in particular, were not celebrating the event. That is due to the massive disappointment in the current leadership of the president Kiir Mayerdit, because they are not doing what they fought for instead they are replicating what we saw under oppressor government (Khartoum regime).

But I stood up strong, and I told them not to lose hope because there are so many positive days ahead! They have to differentiate between president Kiir as a person in charge who might go tomorrow and the country which is there for all of us, and will remain forever.

If you dislike president Kiir's presidency that's is fine, because I do too, but please don't regret that we have our own country for God sake, otherwise, it will be a slap in the face of those martyrs who gave their lives in order for us to enjoy freedom, hope and identity. In that regard, I used my Facebook account, as usual, to tell them this message as follows:

Chapter 23   Lessons for the Future

Do you hate President Kiir's policies or South Sudan as a nation?

My beloved South Sudanese people around the world, I want to take this enormous opportunity to congratulate you all, as we are celebrating our free day.

So, HAPPY SOUTH SUDAN INDEPENDENCE DAY everyone!!!

Yes, I must acknowledge that our sons and daughters have suffered and seen a lot of brutality by their own countrymen since we had our dignity and independence from the most extreme oppressor the world has ever witnessed. I appeal to you all not to lose hope because I have a firm conviction that tomorrow things will be better.

Yes, I must confess that the majority of South Sudanese people are not impressed with President Kiir's divide and rule policies. I ask you to take courage because every story must come to an end and I'm sure one day he will go. Please don't dislike your own country because of him. Yes, I must accept that some South Sudanese people around the world at this moment don't like South Sudan anymore because they don't like President Kiir. That is totally wrong because they're supposed to submit their allegiance to their nation and not to the individual who is in charge. In consideration, they're absolutely entitled to like their president or hate him but the country remains red line and untouchable!

Mr Theodore Roosevelt once said, "Here is your country. Cherish these natural wonders, cherish the natural resources, cherish the history and romance as a sacred heritage, for your children and your children's children. Do not let selfish men or greedy interests skin your country of its beauty, its riches or its romance."

Yes, I have to acknowledge that there are sons and daughters of the South Sudan who think that if President Kiir goes things won't be good for the South Sudan as a country. Those people astonish me because what else is left for us to care about if we lose more lives under President Kiir's leadership than those who paid their blood in order, for us to have this beautiful day called the South Sudan independent day!

PLEASE GIVE US A BREAK!!!

Lastly, I encourage each son and daughter of this beautiful country to refocus on South Sudan as our nation rather than worshipping an individual who won't take us anywhere apart from destruction. Remember we all contributed for the independence of our country, and South Sudan is much bigger than those individuals.

Mr Jesse Ventura once said, "I love my country, not my government."

Thus, I speak louder, that I love my country South Sudan! The question to you is what do you love? Happy South Sudan Independence day!!!!Long live South Sudan!!!

The controversial 28 States of the Republic of South Sudan

In October 2015, South Sudan's President Salva Kiir issued an original decree of establishing 28 states in place of the 10 previously established states. The order formed the new states largely along ethnic lines. On the other hand, the opposition parties challenged the constitutionality of this decree. Despite that, the order was referred to parliament for approval as a constitutional amendment.

In November, the South Sudanese parliament approved the creation of the new states. In January 2017, President Salva Kiir surprised South Sudanese people once again by issuing another decreed of further subdivision of the country from 28 into 32 states. The excuse the president gave out is that he was doing it to implement SPLM's policies of 'taking towns to the people' in the rural areas.

The move was received with mixed reactions. Some citizens praised and welcomed the decree. IGAD and international community narrowly condemned the move and called it a violation of the resolution of the conflict in the Republic of South Sudan, which was signed by President Kiir and rebel leader Dr Reik Machar plus other stakeholders.

From that moment, we heard that there was an intense fight going on in some new states, by people who felt that their land or territory had been taken by the president and given to the other tribe. This was another chaotic environment we found ourselves in which was created by the president. Since then, some intellectuals and myself included, started to raise many questions such as:

Where will the president get the budget?

Why divide the 10 states into 28 states now in particular? What are the reasons behind it?

How will these new states operate with the agreement that was signed based on ten states?

As this continued, I didn't buy the president's idea that he was dividing the country for the development purpose. I was sure he didn't need to do that for him to develop the country, but he was increasing the number of thieves because those who were in charge fail to deliver in ten states which were manageable for him. Now, how on earth, does he think they will perform well in 28 states or more? Additionally, I wasn't happy with the way he divided the country because I didn't know which philosophy or theory he used to split the country that way because I think wider consultation was required on this matter.

I think creating more states will not add anything new to the people apart from more suffering and misfortune. In Australia, there are five states only and two territories, but its facilities are available to everyone.

Moreover, an article which was written in the Briefing Note by the Stimson Center August 9, 2016 amazed me. The article was able to articulate the ramifications of the newly created states wonderfully as following:

a) The 28 states system is causing considerable tension at the national level and is also affecting local conflict dynamics across the country. Former Upper Nile and Western Bahr el Ghazal States are two areas where the 28 states system has already caused significant violence. Conflict in Malakal, has enough potential to destabilise the country.

b) However, it is impossible to generalise about the effects of the 28 states system. In former Lakes State, the system may have decreased inter-communal violence (at least in the short term) by improving local governance.

c) There are many uncertainties about the 28 states system including whether the number of states will remain at 28; what mandate the 15-member review commission will have; What authorities the state leaders will have; whether the new boundaries affect policies related to natural resources; and how the system will be financed.

d) Per the Transitional Constitution, state governors are supposed to be elected; the president has the authority only to appoint 'care-taker' governors. So far, much attention has been focused on whether the SPLM-IO will be given the opportunity to nominate governors for some of the new states, but elections should also be considered when security permits.

e) Reversing the 28 states decision would be complex and could have negative consequences including a popular protest by those who support decentralisation and political opposition by leaders who were appointed under the new system.

Chapter 23 Lessons for the Future

In diaspora particularly in Australia, things were worse because as soon as President Kiir supporters heard the news on South Sudan TV, they didn't waste a minute, they rushed and asked for the divisions of communities in Australia to comply with what the president said. That brought a lot of hatred and conflict amongst so many communities because some have used it for their political gain.

People who refused to comply with president's decree at least abroad with legitimate and logic reasons were accused of betrayal, rebellion and treason for not complying with the order, even though; things are a bit different here.

However, from the bottom of my heart, I thank my South Sudanese mothers especially our Aweilian mothers, for standing affirm and rejecting the divisions of the communities according to what is happening there at home. They confirm our unity. Our mother and elders thank you so much for a terrific job well done!

In South Sudan, the president continued increasing the states from 28 to 32, which means he still has a desire to continue to do that without proper studies and useful strategies. With that being said, I still have a firm conviction that these states will not be there for long because they can't help South Sudan economically, socially and financially. Therefore, they are worth rethinking.

However, Jieng council of elders has been accused of being involved in South Sudan politics, and they became the president's advisers. Therefore, issues such as increasing the numbers of states and dividing them in that manner, plus other issues, were their ideas.

That made me sad because according to the best of my knowledge this branch is not close to politics under any circumstances. To make the matter worse some were proudly acknowledging that work publicly. That irritated the other 63 tribes in South Sudan and they questioned the legality of Jieng's action. As someone from Dinka tribe, who knows this is an unlawful act and it's not helping in terms of the firm unity and peaceful coexistence we are all longing for.

In the meantime, I was blaming the president for allowing such a thing to happen on his watch, knowingly he is not a leader of a particular group or tribe, but he is the president of the entire nation and its 64 tribes. Based on that I wrote this honest and humble article on my Facebook account hoping that it might help:

Why is it difficult for Jieng Council of elders to distance themselves from the president of the Republic?

Jieng Council of elder's roles and activities according to my best understanding, is mainly focused on cultural activities, keeping Dinka tradition and heritage, maintaining Dinka norms and its identity and to make sure they pass it to Dinka next generation.

However, since the conflict erupted in South Sudan 2013, Jieng Council of elders abandoned their cultural role and started to involve in South Sudan politics massively, They became active advisers to the president and their voices have become louder and louder more than ministers and our elected parliamentarians, which raised so many questions:

1. What was the motivation behind their involvement? And why did they get involved so much?

2. Why did the president accept their consultation in the first place?

3. Is their involvement related to South Sudan Constitution to legalise their activities or they are just there because the president is from" Dinka tribe" and they are just there to protect him even though they knew he is part of this senseless war?

Chapter 23 Lessons for the Future

If that is the case, what they will do tomorrow if we have a president from another tribe?

Moreover, the elders of Jieng actually love the job, they are proud of what they have done so far, and that's why they refused to listen to anyone who asked them to stop their work in politics and go back and do cultural activities as they were doing before.

In my opinion, there is no way that "Jieng elders" can tell us that their involvement is logical and meaningful to the sons and daughters of South Sudan. Even though sometimes I don't blame them, but I put my heavy blame on the president of the republic because he shouldn't have worked with them from the beginning and he knew they were only representing "one tribe" amongst 64 tribes.

According to my understanding, the "only" body who has a chance to speak or to advise the president is "South Sudan Council of elders "if we do have that body. Because it is wider and its work can be respected and appreciated by the entire country. Please, our Jieng council of elders let us follow the country's system and the country's Constitution for the sake of this country.

I wrote this powerful message to our Jieng council of elders as small advice that they might stop what they were doing because its consequences are not good for the entire Jieng Community and its reputation and, of course, the nation. I know some Jieng elders might not like this message, and they might take it as a direct insult to them in somehow but this is a truth, and it must be told as I mentioned earlier at the beginning of this book. It must be told to avoid the imminent devastation and collapsing of our beautiful country.

Moreover, me as someone who would love to see peace prevail in my homeland, I was worried and doubting the way both leaders Mr President and the arm opposition leader Dr Reik

Machar approach the implementation of the resolution of the conflict in South Sudan.

Also, as a person who witnessed the devastation of the war in 1983 to 1988 during the Sudan civil war, I was shocked and disappointed to see our men, children and women, humiliated, tortured, dying and suffering again by their own countrymen after we earned our independence after a long struggle from the whole of Sudan.

It is indeed a shameful moment for our leaders to forget easily what they fought for and turned away their focus from our constant enemy. I was furious and angry when I heard from so many news agencies and multiple TV broadcasting that tens of thousands of South Sudanese have been killed by their own countrymen in South Sudan's four year civil war. What a shame! The news sometimes could go beyond imagination by saying that the death in new nation toll much higher than estimates by aid groups that operate in the country and could be even higher than those lost during the war against the Khartoum Islamic regime. This hurt each and every concerned and patriotic citizen, myself included. I wondered and questioned why? Why are we killing ourselves that way? Is that the main reason we fought harder for more than 21 years? Who will be responsible for this meaningless war? And why can't President Kiir and Dr Machar do the honourable thing, the right thing, the decent thing and resign and quit politics completely for the sake of the country and for those who lost their lives in this ungainly war?

Is it having our country at this juncture a cure and is not a blessing? Or, are we proving right what Dr Hassan Al-Turabi who was the major leader of Sudan's Islamic Fundamentalist movement, before we had our independence when he said that: 'Southerners cannot govern themselves.' If that's not the case then why do we see this senseless war after the independence in less than two years?

With that being said, I offer my deepest sorrow, grief, heartbreaking and condolences to those who lost their loved ones on both sides because at the end of the day they are all sons and daughters of this terrific and tremendous country.

However, I kept writing on my Facebook account every day since the conflict erupted back home because I was trying to put pressure on both leaders. President Kiir and his former vice president Riek Machar that they might disregard their personal interest and their group interest and contribute fully and bring real peace to the country. Every day I was writing because nothing else occupied my head apart from how can this awkward war come to an end? Because it worried me, and I kept asking myself, where will this conflict lead South Sudan to? Most of my messages, I typically directed them to the president because he is the head of the state; therefore, I wanted him to do more. That's why I wrote this article:

Exactly what kind of peace does President Kiir want in South Sudan?

Last year President Kiir signed the resolution of the conflict of the Republic of South Sudan with too many reservations, more than the agreement itself. Those reservations were rejected immediately afterwards by IGAD and the international community.

From that time president, Kiir started to implement the peace agreement the way he wanted, abandoning the part he doesn't want, using the delay tactics on the part he doesn't want and breaching part of agreement that doesn't accommodate his interests and his wishes. For example, when he created 28 states, and he knew it was wrong and absolutely inconsistent with the peace agreement that he personally signed.

Moreover, last July he used what they call "divide and rule policy" by appointing Taban Deng Gai as "FVP" and he knew very well the guy was dismissed by Dr. Riek Machar, but he was sure and confident and knew exactly what he was doing? The list of political manipulation and fraudulent acts from his Excellency continues, while southerners still don't get it yet!

However, above all, President Kiir claimed he is a man of peace after all of these tactics and hypocrisy which are absolutely against peace and stability of any country around the world because they provoke and blackmail the opposition side without a doubt.

Lastly, I think the peace the president meant is different from the one we are normally preaching or hoping for, President Kiir doesn't want any "opposition" in South Sudan because he wants to establish a kingdom in South Sudan by showing no interest of relinquishing the presidency so far, otherwise he would implement the peace agreement by spirit and letter so that the reform and accountability can take place toward a prosperous, stable, peaceful and democratic South Sudan. One that we can be proud of. And 'please stop pretending.'

The returning of some South Sudanese back to Khartoum after things turned ugly in their new country

Since this horrifying and deadly war within ourselves started, many South Sudanese lost everything, and were forced to run to the neighbouring countries such as Sudan, Uganda, Kenya, Democratic of Congo and Ethiopia. Those who returned to Sudan, many of them are from my own hometown Aweil. They returned, as they had no other option. Otherwise, they would die of hunger and deadly diseases, as the situation in the country was turning awful! So many people are losing their lives every day; either by hunger or deadly disease or being killed by both forces president Kiir's forces and opposition group forces.

In Khartoum, some South Sudanese were welcomed back, the rest were not according to sources such as friends, news agencies and some family's members who decided to go back to Sudan. According to what we were told so far by those who are

Chapter 23 Lessons for the Future

living there and Sudan, South Sudan Government is that those who returned to the Khartoum Sudan had been put in refugee camps outside the city. The government of Sudan even though they are doing a great job to help the refugees from my country South Sudan, at the same time they are trying hard to humiliate and denigrate them. By naming their camps with names such; Malish which means (Sorry for coming back), Ja'biraw means (come back by himself) and so on. It pains me most because I knew the Arabic language very well and understood those terms and what they meant. It is absolutely disgraceful! With that being said, the general situation is remarkable, and many people have been put back to their work. Others have been told that they are happy to see you back even though we didn't know why you left in the first place? That has made me wonder that until now some brothers and sisters from North Sudan, still didn't get yet why we separated from the Mother Sudan!

Regarding Atak Ken Agany's family, some went back to Khartoum as I wasn't able to support them all financially. My mother, two brothers and two sisters, Athain Atak Ken and his family decided to remain in the country. Mother said that enough is enough and I'm not going back Sudan under any circumstance because I'm so tired. In the meantime, she said that she is not blaming those who went back to Khartoum because people are facing extreme hunger or lethal disease.

In my own opinion, I felt sorry for those who went back to Sudan in less than five years since we gained our independence from them. I knew it was a challenging period for my fellow South Sudanese who went back to Khartoum after they said goodbye to the Khartoum City, four years ago. Some people were dancing and singing the songs of goodbye in their own languages to express their happiness and gladness that they are going to their real home country after long suffering and injustices to go back again to the same place. Regrettably, this time is not going to be like the last time when they were treated as Sudanese. This time they were treated as foreigners, in other words, Sudan is no longer their country.

My message to the Sudanese people and to their Government is that they have to treat these returnees with respect and dignity because I'm confident we as South Sudanese, we will overcome this mess and we will be a strong country in east Africa, mark my word. What is happening right now, it has to occur for us to learn the enormous lesson of loving our country and work hard for its success and development. I have Great Spirit and believe that we will overcome this tragedy and put our differences aside and follow the rules of law and constitution. Yes, we did take refuge in Sudan in our first war with the oppressor Khartoum regime plus other neighbouring countries. We did it again today in our own meaningless and unjustified war among ourselves. Once again, mark my word after we overcome this unreasonable conflict we won't take refuge again in any country. In fact, it is Sudanese from the north's turn because since we left, their house hasn't been in order or peaceful. It seems it is not going to be soon, because they still didn't change their mentality and mistreatment that made us leave the entire Sudan 6 years ago.

In my normal life in Western Australia I continue to struggle and suffer severely financially, despite that, I'm working as a full-time employee at Vesco Foods in Osborne Park. It happened due to the huge family responsibility on my shoulder. So, as usual, I'm in charge of taking care of my own family here by paying rent every fortnight and high price bills every two months, paying for food items plus other required family expenditures are fully my certain responsibilities.

My car is getting old, and therefore, it is costing me a lot of money by having to do repairs from time to time. I should have upgraded it by now with a better newer model, according to the mechanics reports. Unfortunately, I cannot afford it. Due to some difficulties in saving money, because my expenditures are too high, in other words, I'm living right now beyond my means

Chapter 23 Lessons for the Future

to the extent that sometimes I cannot afford to pay for petrol. I remembered last month I went to the petrol station to buy fuel. Remarkably! After I had got the fuel, I was embarrassed while I was trying to pay the price, because my bankcard didn't work for the cashier to get his $30 AUD. I had an insufficient amount of funds in my account and I didn't know that. That forced me to park the car, walk back home and try to get the money. So I walked from Mirrabooka petrol station to my home address in Balga. I reached my home in about 15 minutes. Thank God my wife helped me out by giving me $30 AUD she put away for something else, but she had no choice but to give it to me so that I could walk back and claim my car back. It seems difficult financial situations cannot leave me no matter what. This is absolutely what happened? Personally, I didn't like the situation, but there was nothing in my power I could do so I took it easy and moved on stronger, confident and better equipped than before, and I still have an unpredictable passion for life. Life is inconsistent. Today is challenging and tomorrow is easy, or today feeling sad and sorry, tomorrow is pleasant and joyful!

However, due to the worsening situation in my home country, the South Sudanese people working at Vesco foods, were challenged last year by an Arab person who had recently arrived from Khartoum. When he said that South Sudanese chose the wrong path by deciding to separate from the whole Sudan, therefore, they are supposed to reunite the country again, for them to be able to survive, otherwise, they all will die slowly if they don't pay enough attention. After we heard that from him, we condemned him terribly with the definite term and rejected the ideas. I told him personally that myself and other South Sudanese around the world, we voted confidently to separate the South. We did that with pride and honour after we knew that it was tough for us to live with you together in one country due to deep mistrust and unimaginable injustice we witnessed for so many decades.

If today we couldn't manage our own affairs properly, then put in mind that it is better for us to die, but no chance of reuniting the country again man. I told him honestly that all these hardships and misfortunes would go away. One day we will have a peaceful and prosperous nation that can accommodate all of us.

Additionally, despite all these challenges, I still support my mother financially all the time, Athian Mapher and his family and the other families sometimes. On 12.08.2017, I introduced Mr Athian Mapher to my friends on Facebook for the first time by telling them who he is and the enormous role that he has played in my life. I presented him so amazingly and wonderfully and by writing about how good he was and singing his praises that it impressed so many friends.

With that being said I wrote the following:

Ladies and gentlemen my fellow South Sudanese people this is my brother Athian Atak Ken Agany. He is also well-known as Athian Mapher Atak Ken.

However, for everyone's information, without this man's outstanding effort, I wouldn't be where I am today without him.

Athian Atak Ken Agany is not only an excellent brother to me, but he is a friend, mentor and my role model and if and when I become a famous and influential figure tomorrow in our society, then it is because of his tremendous encouragement and extraordinary support. Once again, Ladies and gentlemen, this is phenomenal Mr Athian Mapher Atak Ken!!!

As soon as I had written this on my Facebook home page I have been congratulated by so many friends on Facebook for having such a terrific and good brother like Athian at this difficult moment. I thanked them so much and took all their comments as compliments from them.

Chapter 23   Lessons for the Future

Being an influential community member, I participate in all the meetings and community decision-making processes to make our community fantastic and spectacular not only for us, but also for the next generation. This year, which is 2017, I was elected for the reviewing of both constitutions. The local one called Aweil Community constitution in Western Australia and Mading Aweil Community Constitution in Australia (MAC) at large with Mr James Jhok Atuer. Thanked God we were able to do the both jobs successful even though it wasn't easy at all.

Moreover, MAC Australia is our umbrella where Aweil sons and daughters meet every year in one state to share their issues and embrace unity and togetherness. In one of the best and tremendous social atmospheres, every active member can dream of!

This year was organised in South Australia, but unfortunately, I couldn't make it to the meeting due to financial difficulties. But those who went, did a great job and elected Mr Simon Henry Angok to be our president for the second term after he had many successes in his first term.

Therefore, as a member of Aweil community I took a chance and used my Facebook home page and wrote the following message to Mr Angok and his outstanding team as followings:

!!!!!!!!!!!!!!!!!!!Congratulatory Message!!!!!!!!!!!!!!!!!!!

My beloved Aweil community members across Australia; I want to take this opportunity to congratulate Mr Simon Henry Angok, for being elected as President of Mading Aweil Community in Australia (MAC) for the second term. In my opinion, Mr Angok did a great job. Therefore, he deserves another two years. Many congratulations Mr President!!

I want to use this chance also to congratulate our Aweil mothers across Australia for standing up with one voice for the Unity of Mading Aweil across Australia. Our women, sisters and mothers from the bottom of my heart I wish you well and good health to be able to continue to do what you are doing right now. Congratulations for an enormous job well done!

With honour and respect, I congratulate our elders and state community leaders for keeping Aweil community as one body in whole Australia despite massive opposition, which is desperate to destroy this beautiful unity. To our elders! Might God bless you all and give you strength and health.

Mr Simon, the floor is yours to provide a good atmosphere for everyone to contribute effectively. With that said, please try to be president for those who stood for you when you needed them and those who didn't. Be a president to those who are seeking for the unity of Mading Aweil to continue and thrive and chair for those who pray day in and day out to see this terrific unity ruin.

Remember, to teach your team in office to work as one unit, because I have a firm conviction that by doing so you will do a magnificent job, Mr Mattie Stepanek once said, "Unity is a strength... when there is teamwork and collaboration, wonderful things can be achieved".

Once again, I congratulate you Mr Simon for winning the trust of Mading Aweil Members across Australia. You did a lot already, and I'm sure you will do more in this term. Mr Abraham Lincoln once said in one of his best quote ever, "Nearly all men can stand adversity, but if you want to test a man's character, give him power".

Long live Aweil Community in our States in Australia

Long live Mading Aweil Community in Australia (MAC)

In response to this congratulatory message. Aweil sons and daughters around the world were delighted and amazed with this congratulatory message, and they thanked me for doing that excellent job. It would be fantastic if they see me at our

Chapter 23 Lessons for the Future

next General Assembly meeting (AGM), which will take place in Melbourne, Victoria next year 2018, they said. I agreed, and I'm preparing myself right now, even though it is too early for that.

This year we celebrated Mother's Day in our parish at St. Bakhita Catholic church, Westminster, Perth, Western Australia as usual. We did that in one of the best ways ever, and our priest Sam was absolutely phenomenal. That day he gave one of the best sermons ever. On that day, Father Sam told an entire congregation an excellent story about a mother and his 'naughty boy'.

He said that there was a naughty boy who didn't like to be asked to do something for himself or anybody else. He didn't even do things for his mother and complained about everything. One day his mother told him; my son you are a little bit older, and I think the time is right for you now to start learning and practise how to do your own stuff.

No worries mother I will do that, but are you going to pay me for that job? If yes then how much are you going to give me for doing my own stuff? The boy replied.

Then he took some paper, and he started to write:

For me to wake up early every day, you have to pay me $5, mother.

To have a shower, brush my teeth every day in the morning, which is a little bit harder for me. Therefore, you will give me $15 for just doing that job.

To do my homework, work hard diligently in class and make sure I do well in school, that one is even more challenging than you think mother. You have to pay me $50. The total amount is $70 every month, mother.

Then he gave this paper to his mother.

What! Where am I going to get $70 every month for my son? mother questions.

Then his mother took the paper from him and turned the paper, and she started to write on the back of the paper.

She wrote:

I carried you in my womb for more than 9 months; the cost was $0.

When I gave birth, I didn't sleep because you were so naughty and you kept crying throughout the night. The cost for that job as well was $0.

Changing your nappies and washing your dirty clothes every day, the cost was also $0.

If you get sick for example, I took you to hospital pay for your medicine, and I cannot eat or feel comfortable until you get well, the cost for that was $0. The total cost was $0.

Then the mother gave the paper back to his son. At that moment the boy burst into tears. Thanks mother for taking care of me. Now I know you love me so much.

It was an incredible story on Mother's day. All parents in the church were happy and delighted to hear that fabulous and emotional story, particularly on that day.

Politically, I committed myself to read all the news that updates us about the situation in my beloved South Sudan. The reputable news agencies that I trust to give me an actual information every day are Sudan Tribune, South Sudan news agency, Radio Tamazuj, BBC, CNN and All Africa. Therefore, I want to take this opportunity to thank them all for the outstanding job they are doing every day because without them it would be tough to know what is going on particularly when things turned very nasty in the country. With that being said, I know very well that

Chapter 23 Lessons for the Future

they were accused many times by the government of the South Sudan that they are spreading negative news and misleading the public in and outside the country without providing accurate evidence to back it up. That is normal because my government is not used to that kind of pressure, but with time they will be fine. Private news agencies are significant for the accuracy and transparency of the report.

However, what I saw at the beginning of the conflict, what I read from news and watched from SSTV I realised that South Sudan is heading into a difficult period.

Added to that, both president's supporters and Dr Machar's supporters are spreading and preaching hatred speeches and disunity songs. Since that period there has been nothing in social media such as Facebook, apart from insisting hatred among the one nation.

As a concerned citizen, I did my part by warning them that they have to be cautious and act responsibly. Regrettably, no one was ready to listen because people were divided to 'Machar's supporters "and "Kiir's supporters" and they left the REPUBLIC OF THE SOUTH SUDAN to suffer alone.

Both leaders, according to my analyses, all murdered and killed south Sudanese people. Therefore, it didn't matter which one you support. In the end, we are losing vulnerable and fragile people here and no leader is ready to show any sign of compromise.

Starting with President Kiir who did his work in Juba in the genesis of this conflict and Mr Machar did the rest in Upper Nile by claiming that his tribe has been massacred in Juba, these are factors, and absolutely no leader is "clean" in this war there's no good guy.

If I were both Cams, they are supposed to stop that attitudes and give peace and reconciliation a chance. We can then start to rebuild our nation once again and remember, taking aside and standing with your tribe won't help and denying the facts will complicate the situation.

I'm also encouraging my fellow South Sudanese that they have to talk for the sake of this country because if we choose to keep quiet it won't help at all. Martin Luther King once said: "Our lives begin to end the day we become silent about things that matter".

So let us talk and discuss important issues without fear or intimidation from anybody. This is our country, and it is we alone who have to fix this mess, no one else. Therefore, people should preach forgiveness, peace and love as the only way to move forward.

Mr Martin Luther King also said, "Love is the only force capable of transforming an enemy into a friend." This is so true, therefore, the real challenging question to all south Sudanese around the world is. Can we embrace and comply with this quote for the sake of our beloved South Sudan?

For the president, it is a wonder we are not seeing him addressing the nation regularly, telling them that it's important for them to focus on their country, not him or Reik Machar.

Therefore, I wrote a strong message on my Facebook account hoping he will find it and do something about it. I put it this way:

Why doesn't President Kiir address the issue of the patriotism and nationalism to his people?

The real leaders, they shine and lustre their toughness and strength in crisis and in the critical moment like the one that we're living in since 2013, by trying to carry all his people on his shoulder without anyone, being left out.

Since the conflict started in South Sudan three years ago. A lot of South Sudanese people and myself included, expected his

Chapter 23 Lessons for the Future

Excellency the president of the Republic of the South Sudan to come out and address his people about "nationalism and nativism" and tell them how we got this "beautiful country" as one tribe and one nation.

President Kiir as commander-in-chief has enormous responsibilities and obligations to speak to people's hearts and keep them onside, why we fought for more than 21 years and now who is our real constant enemy?

However, I'm saying this because nowadays, southerners are worshipping and adoring their own tribes and forgot about their main real identity, one (South Sudanese).

They showed to the whole world how loyalist they are in terms of favouring their tribes.

If our president lacks the talent to convince us, then we are indeed in deep trouble.
South Sudanese people abroad should live above their tribes, regions and ethnicities

I arrived here in Western Australia in 2005, and I found South Sudanese Community more united than ever. They celebrate 16th May every year together. 16th May is a significant day in South Sudan History because it is the day SPLA/ SPLM as a rebel movement was formed on 16th May 1983, after the Sudan government's abandonment of the Addis Ababa agreement signed between the Gaafar Nimeiry government and the Anyanya leader Joseph Lagu. Since then 16thMay became a "historic day" in South Sudan history. A day that represents the interests of the marginalised communities in the history of the old Sudan, that period including Blue Nile, Abyei and Nuba Mountains.

After we lost Dr Garang, we all came together as one and condemned the move. In fact, some went beyond and considered his particular death as an assassination, due to the circumstances that surrounded his unexpected death that shocked millions of South Sudanese around the world.

Also, we fought hard together to have a referendum and when we had it, we voted overwhelmingly for separation of the South. Since then we used to celebrate our independence together again as one people. However, after the 'nightmare' of 15th December 2013 we failed badly to keep and preserve that unity. South Sudanese Australians, those who are living abroad in particular, started to divide themselves according to their clan and horde.

But, the real question is, did any tribe come out victorious?

I don't think so. But what I do know is that we all contributed heavily to the destruction of a country which didn't exceed five years old since its independence. We proved to the whole world that our little ethnicities blood is much thicker than the blood of Christ. What a shame!

Therefore, our involvement we as people who are leaving abroad are supposed to be a positive and peaceful voice, not the other way around. Citizens in South Sudan expect a lot from us, but we proved them completely wrong. What a huge disappointment!

The history of the country will not forgive us. It will record that we failed badly to manage our own affairs after we gained our nation from the whole Sudan. It is discreditable!

However, we as South Sudanese who are living overseas, in particular, we have a big responsibility to reconcile those who are fighting in the country right now. We saw how the world could benefit from the diversity. It helps for the devolvement of the country. Countries that are multicultural societies such; Australia, Canada etc. demonstrated to us perfectly!

The country where everyone is a politician and wants to be a president!

Chapter 23 Lessons for the Future

If there is anyone, out there who still doubts and wonders that there is no country in the world where every citizen is practising politics and doing his/her utmost to be a politician. Seek actively the several ways that can take him/her to the presidency, and then guess what my beloved South Sudan is!

I have to acknowledge, and my countrymen and women should agree with me on this, that since we had our lovely country, I saw my fellow South Sudanese people around the world are increasingly involved massively in politics and forgot about other aspects that their country might require their attention. They are all pretending to be called genuine politicians, other than that it is considered as insulting to them, with respect to our real politicians. It is quite astonishing isn't it? To see the entire nation with the same desire and passion just to do one job and follow only one carrier! Even though it is not what their country needs.

A newborn country such as ours which needs everything to speed up the process of development and prosperity not only in one field such as politics and Government. We fought with determination and outstanding effort to have this country, therefore, we should continue to do so, to make our country great in all aspects, not just focusing on one thing.

We are supposed to encourage, train ourselves and our next generation in whatever professions and skills we may have available. For example, people should study and work harder to become doctors, nurses, teachers, scientists, lawyers, engineers and agriculturalists etc.

So, there is no excuse for us starting to engage ourselves slowly in politics, despite that some of us are not qualified to be politicians. It is remarkable because so many people are wondering and asked where did we get this same attribute? Is it because of long suffering and unacceptable oppression that we went through during struggle time? Or is it because we were created that way *naturally? Is it because there is a lacking of jobs and private sectors? What pains me most, is that it seems to me that we are not going to change this path of engaging in politics only and disregarding the rest. So many South Sudanese students inside and outside the country are doing courses that are related to politics and leadership, political science courses, international relation courses etc.*

They are doing these courses with only one goal in mind and that is to become a politician or a president, if there is any chance. Those students who are not following that path and are doing different courses which are not related to politics such as; construction courses, medicine, sciences etc. are not getting that much support or enough attention in the wider community.

What my fellow citizens should know is that they have to change this unacceptable mentality, for the beneficiaries of the country, which means we must associate ourselves with the numerous and various social and cultural organisations, whereby we can have the opportunity to learn and practise different things apart from politics.

I'm confident that by involving ourselves in new paths and new ways of thinking, we shall be more active and know the facts of life and what our country needs most. That kind of approach is very significant for our nation building. Politics should be left to a few and the rest should start now, not later to build schools for children, hospitals, roads, bridges, community centres for awareness and education, recreation centres to promote our incredible cultures and traditions not only in Juba but across the country.

The prosperity of our nation and its development depends on us. No-one will come and do it for us if we cannot do that. Every citizen has an enormous role to play in nation building and sustainability of the nation. The powerful countries like the

Chapter 23 Lessons for the Future

United States of America, where many people love to visit to spend their holidays and vacations. It wasn't built by angels but has been constructed by her dedicated and committed citizens who work hard to make it great. Therefore we can do that for our country. Nothing is impossible in this world; as Nelson Mandela put it that, "it always seems impossible until it's done".

From that point, I could say that there are so many ways for people around the world, not only in South Sudan to serve their country. On the other hand, the Government of South Sudan should invest and support our students who are doing science, mining, engineering etc. and prepare them to be our engineers and scientists. It is a duty and obligation of any government to provide that kind of support and assistance to its students. Students and my fellow citizens, let us not waste time in one area such as politics which will take the rest nowhere at the end of the day. We should start to be more creative to think critically by defining ourselves and what we can do best as an individual for us to contribute for constructive and building our country, and stop our next generation from possible suffering.

However, there is nothing wrong with our students doing politics courses or something similar to it, nor it is a crime of dreaming of being a president of your country. However, they should be aware that position of the presidency is only "one" in the whole country, there is no room to accommodate more than one person, and only a few are lucky to get it.

According to my analysis, I think this is one of the problems why our country is not in peace since we had it. My fellow citizen's ambitions to reach that position is so high. While on another hand, president Kiir and his subordinates are ready to die before they let that title go away from them. This is the general situation right now in the country if I'm not wrong? So, every citizen, in the country, is seeking to be a parliamentarian, Governor or a minster if not the president. Even though he/she is not capable or qualify to hold these positions.

I think our intellectuals have to do some awareness and education across the country to the majority of the citizens to inform them that politics is not only the job in the nation they can have. There are so many significant jobs that the country can provide and so desperately need to have people on it. My fellow citizens should know that we are looking for doctors, engineers and pharmacists etc. These are the jobs South Sudan need urgently right now more than ever. Therefore, we have to change this unwise mentality. If we cannot change that attitude then the future of our country will be unpredictable. We have to love our country and work hard for its development by offering the greatest service we can give to the nation, which killed more than two million people.

I am writing this book for the community and wider audience, to have a lasting record of my life's journey. I'm also writing this book to inform and illustrate to the world how we as South Sudanese people endured extreme discrimination, brutality, injustice, humiliation, mistreatment and segregation under Khartoum Islamic regime government and Egyptian people especially, South Sudanese who sought refuge in Egypt. I'm sure the world might spotlight some unacceptable behaviours that have the right of the Southerners in Sudan at the oppression period. They fail badly to record and reveal the hardship and unspeakable discrimination we as South Sudanese experienced at the hands of that country that called itself the 'mother of the world'!

As for my beloved South Sudan people, this is my first book and the second book will be purely political I guarantee you. In addition, I won't stop writing until my government in Juba cease to replicate the same mistake that Khartoum has committed against its own citizens. I know there are many people out there who may be more intellectual or better educated than me, but they may choose to keep quiet. As for me, I won't do that because doing nothing is not an option at all. Mr Elbert Hubbard once said if you don't want to be criticised don't say anything, do nothing and be nothing'.

My message to the people of South Sudan, the politicians and their supporters is that they must have loyalty and pledge to the Constitution and the rule of law. They should not allow, under any circumstance for both to be compromised by anyone, not even the president himself. Another message to the South Sudanese community around the world, and that is they should be careful about their daily activities and behaviours because according to my small experiences' what you do today whether it is good deeds or evil, our evil deeds will come back to you tomorrow.' That is why they say, what goes around comes around!

I am still a young man, and I still have many things ahead of me. One of my dreams is to serve my people one day, in the Republic of South Sudan. In saying that, I won't stop writing. I will try to be a voice for those who are voiceless. I will use every space and every minute I have to express my strong opinion to the world, particularly my fellow South Sudanese people. I will keep using my Facebook account, email account, Twitter, Messenger, Google account and even text message if I can. I am encouraging my fellow citizens to do the same and not to lose the moral and motivation at all. Otherwise, this suffering of our people back home won't stop. Vince Lombardi once said; if you aren't fired with enthusiasm, you will be fired with enthusiasm".

Adut Jok Aher

I think that it will be a mistake, as I'm writing this book, not to mention our great musician Adut Jok Aher and her pleasing songs. We, as Dinka community and Aweil community have been blessed by our lovely singer Athok Jok Aher and her wonderful songs.

I believe she is the greatest young singer from South Sudan ever! I listen to her songs every day before I go to work through YouTube and Facebook. She has impressed both myself and my little boy Agany Deng Atak who also loves her music.

Adut is young, brilliant and beautiful and the best musician this generation has produced so far, and that has made us proud. Actually, she has so many songs, and they are all amazing and wonderful! In saying that, I used my Facebook home page to express my delightedness and gladness with her songs, and I wrote the followings on date 15.06.2017,

Acknowledging and appreciating the magnificent work of our incredible Singer Athokjok Adut Jok Aher!!!

My beloved South Sudanese people around the globe, please join me to congratulate our great young singer Athokjok Adut Aher for her outstanding and meaningful songs!

Athokjok we thank you so much for your fantastic songs and being able to win hearts of many South Sudanese people around the world particularly those who can understand Dinka language.

Ladies and gentlemen after we lost our great musician of all times Nyankol Mathiang, many people lost hope, myself included, and we thought we would never have another great singer like her.

But we thank God for giving us another wonderful gift called "Athokjok." Adut Aher might God give you strength and good health to be able to continue doing what you are doing right now.

Long live Mading Aweil,

Long live Yirol

Long live our spectacular singer Athokjok Adut Jok Aher

Photo Album

This was me when I was in Egypt, 2004.

*This is my mother,
Abuk Mayol Amoi Lual, Khartoum 2004.*

*This is my brother Mr Athain Atak Ken Agany.
Well known as Athain Mapher.*

Chapter 23   Photo Album

This is Elizibeth Sama Mawein and her husband Mr Tamim Abdulrahman

My friend Mr Thiik Deng Riing and I, South Australia 2009.

This wonderful picture was taken while I was doing my job at St.Bakhita Catholic church as one of the liturgical organisers and chorister.

Former SPLM general secretary Pagan Amum Okiech and I when he visited W.A

Chapter 23   Photo Album

The Perth Commissioner, myself and Mr Chan Aweech at the citizenship ceremony

Mr Karlo Ken Ken, my brother Agany Atak Ken, my wife Abuk Kuach and I.

Chapter 23 Photo Album

My wife Abuk Kuach Ngor and I, March 2013.

My lovely wife Abuk Kuach

My Son Agany Deng Atak Ken, 2016

Chapter 23   Photo Album

Chapter 23   Photo Album

Mr Malith Makuc Kual and I at Sarah Abdelbagi's wedding.

This beautiful picture was taken at Sarah Abdelbagi's wedding.

Deng Atak Ken

www.ingramcontent.com/pod-product-compliance
Lightning Source LLC
Chambersburg PA
CBHW031414290426
44110CB00011B/376